WHAT PEOPLE ARE S...

"Brandon and I have now journeyed together for over 15 years and he has never ceased to amaze me. Without exaggeration, I have trained and coached tens of thousands of people in the last 30+ years, and Brandon stands out among the best of them. I have never seen a man of his age so well-read, well-spoken and accomplished in leading powerful people. Brandon makes me proud."

- JOEL SCRIVNER
4X World Champion, Executive Coach, Pastor,
Founder and Author of WINology

"Brandon's life story of overcoming obstacles will inspire you to evaluate and improve the way you respond to challenges in life. He is a man that has not run from trials but has embraced them in an effort to increase his value and maximize his impact. If you want to know who God created you to be and how He wants to use you, keep this book in your library to read again and again..."

- STEPHEN HAYES
Senior Pastor of Covenant Church

"Recognizing Your Value is one of those books that can be a game changer for someone trying to figure out who they are. So many people spend years, and even decades, trying to find their voice and their lane—but I believe in this book, Brandon gives his audience the tools, not only to know who they are but WHY they are. Brandon has a unique writing style that keeps the reader engaged at a high level. This book is important for everyone to read."

- RYAN LEAK
Renowned Speaker and Author of UnOffendable

"Brandon is an inspiring young leader with the wisdom of a seasoned veteran. He has an innate ability to capture profound truths and relate them in clear, often humorous ways. Through captivating real-life stories and his own amazing journey in recognizing the value he brings to the world—this book will help you see value in yourself that maybe you never saw or discounted before and to see your challenges as opportunities to grow and crush obstacles. **The world around you is waiting for you to be all you were created to be, Recognizing Your Value will help you get there!***"*

- CLINT HATTON
Leader, Coach, and Communicator

"Brandon's story is one of hope and strength! His insight on life is refreshing in a world of negativity. **You'll be moved and encouraged to keep fighting in the midst of the struggle!***"*

- CREG DARBY
Associate Youth Pastor at Covenant Church

Recognizing YOUR VALUE

The Traits In Your Life That Will Set You Apart

BRANDON COX

RECOGNIZING YOUR VALUE

© 2019 by Brandon Cox

Second Edition: March 2019

Printed in the United States of America
Edited by Amy Noelck

To my wife, Angelmarie.
You are the half that has made me whole.
My greatest friend, my relentless encourager, my love for
eternity. You are the light of my life. If I lived 100
lifetimes, I would marry you each time.

CONTENTS

FOREWORD

I'll never forget the first time Brandon Cox came up on my radar. I was assisting in coaching the varsity soccer team for American Heritage Academy, a small private school where I served as a Bible teacher, chaplain, and mentor. There were quite a few students who came out for the team. Some were highly skilled in "the beautiful game," as it is called around the world, while others lacked soccer experience, but made up for it in guts and grit. Brandon, a natural basketball player, struck me as the latter.

Brandon was a tall, lean, 14-year-old freshman, with hair like Elvis and the swagger to match. At the time, I was thirty, only recently retired from my professional martial arts career, and still in pretty sassy physical condition. As the volunteer assistant coach, I made it my goal to run, drill, and scrimmage with the team (and be the "old man" who yelled, screamed, and pushed them to try and keep up).

On one specific occasion, as I was driving toward the goal, Brandon stepped up to the challenge. I threw my hip and shoulder into him, with a little extra pepper, and secretly enjoyed watching him tumble to the turf. As I dribbled past him, I laughingly chided, "Suck it up, freshman!" Not to be cruel, but to intentionally provoke him. I wanted to see what was in him. To my delight, that skinny freshman bounded to his feet in relentless, hot pursuit—and with no shortage of his own version of teen trash talk. I totally dug it. But truly, what makes this story so sweet in my memory is that it was only a few short weeks later, in a similar soccer skirmish, it was I who found myself looking up at Brandon with my back on the pitch. Touché.

Brandon Cox is a fighter: tenacious, determined, stubborn, brilliant, resilient, focused, driven, and uniquely confident. Brandon has made a distinct and unforgettable mark on my life. When Brandon finished high school, he took me to lunch to interview me. *The result?* He decided that I had made the cut and accepted my invitation to become my intern. Brandon dedicated 30 hours a week toward working with me for two years, while he finished his college degree in three years and still managed to juggle a world-class social life.

Brandon and I have now journeyed together for over 15 years and he has never ceased to amaze me. Without exaggeration, I have trained and coached tens of thousands of people in the last 30+ years, and Brandon stands out among the best of them. I have never seen a man of his age so well-read, well-spoken and accomplished in leading powerful people. Brandon makes me proud. Of all the people I know to write a book on "Recognizing Your Value," Brandon is uniquely qualified. His deep insight, gift of story, and innate ability to captivate and inspire have enabled him to create a powerfully written work that is sure to challenge, provoke, engage, and inspire. This is a book you must read again and again.

- JOEL SCRIVNER

INTRODUCTION

RECOGNIZING YOUR VALUE

I heard an interesting story recently. Someone had a winning lottery ticket that was never cashed in. The winning set of numbers on the ticket was worth $77 million! The winner got the difficult part right by picking the correct numbers, but for reasons unexplained, the person never came by to pick up the winnings. The deadline came and went. Midnight struck. The ticket went from being worth millions of dollars to being a useless piece of paper. All because the winner never got up and claimed what was theirs.

Potential has a brief shelf life. It has an expiration date that is approaching. Your calling and opportunities in life aren't a Twinkie. Like milk, fruit, and vegetables, it won't keep forever. It can spoil and go bad. The works and achievements that are designed for your life will pass you by if you don't take hold of them.[1]

Mark Twain once told a story about a man who searched the planet looking for the greatest general who had ever lived. When the man was informed that the person he sought had already died and gone to heaven, he made a trip to the Pearly Gates to look for him. Saint Peter pointed at a regular-looking Joe and the man protested, "This isn't the greatest of generals! I knew that person when he lived on the earth, and he was only a cobbler."

"I know that," Saint Peter replied, "but if he had been a general, he would have been the greatest of them all."[2]

One of the most important discoveries in life is recognizing the value within yourself. Sadly, it seems that most people never come to that realization. Or if they do, they start working on the potential they have but don't finish what they have started. It's easy to start, but hard to finish. Few can believe and persevere for as long as it takes to become successful.

Many people have started on a new goal or project in an effort to make their dream a reality. It can be easy to lose motivation when life gets tough. You have to make a conscious decision to be tough. When life gets tough, the tough get going. Motivation is also key, but it's a daily exercise we need to practice. Zig

Ziglar said it best, "People often say that motivation doesn't last. Well, neither does bathing. That's why we recommend it daily."

Recently, I spoke on a Sunday morning at my church discussing the importance of investing in others. When the service was finished, I walked down the steps from the platform and began making my way to the lobby to meet and greet the people who had attended that day. Before I made it to the lobby, I was stopped by an elderly gentleman slowly coming my way with his cane in hand. He introduced himself and told me that he enjoyed hearing me speak. He complimented me and with a sparkle in his eye, he said, "Make sure and finish what you've started. Keep going, young man."

Though his compliment was simple, it was sincere and it encouraged me to continue pursuing what I feel God has placed on my life. These small moments often catapult us into our destiny. They will shape our future if we allow them to. This man's compliment reminded me of my potential.

Potential is God's gift to us. What we do with it is our gift to Him. There is great value in you, but it's up to you to recognize it.

PART I

YOU'VE GOT THE GOODS

CHAPTER ONE

YOU ARE VALUABLE

"If you think you are too small to be effective,
you have never been in the dark with a mosquito."

- Betty Reese

Everyone wants to own things of value, but it seems as though too few of us feel valuable on our own two feet.

One of the things that can help our self-esteem, or how we feel about ourselves, is when other people compliment us. Specifically, when someone you admire speaks up and gives you encouragement about what they see in you.

As a Christian, I believe that God made you. He designed you. You are His idea.

He thought about your personality.

The color of your hair.

What type of body you would have.

The parents you would be born to.

The neighborhood you would live in.

The talents and passion you would possess.

And what you would enjoy doing in your spare time.

It is wild to think that the Creator of the universe thinks about us on a personal level. We often wonder, *If He's God, isn't He too busy for me?* But it is because He is God that He is able to live outside of time and space. He enjoys every minute and every detail of your life and who you are. I believe He takes pleasure in that. He takes pleasure in creating, seeing, and knowing you. King David thought about the same things mentioned above, and his mind was blown away by the concept. He writes about it in Psalm 139:13-18:

"You made all the delicate, inner parts of my body and knit me together in my mother's womb. Thank you for making me so wonderfully complex! Your workmanship is marvelous—how well I know it. You watched me as I was being formed in utter seclusion, as I was woven together in the dark of the womb. You saw me before I was born. Every day of my life was recorded in your book. Every moment was laid out before a single day had passed. How precious are your thoughts about me O God. They cannot be numbered! I can't even count them; they outnumber the grains of sand! And when I wake up, you are still with me!"

2

God created you with value. If you are valuable to Him, you are valuable to the world as well. Your life is your story and your story has a purpose. And I think it's about time we recognize the value that we possess.

Let's Fight!

I was an only child growing up. I loved roughhousing and wrestling with my dad. It was playful in nature, but I have always been very competitive as well. My dad says that as a little kid, I would come up to him with my fists raised and a smile on my face saying, "Let's fight!" We made a lot of good memories doing that. But sometimes we would get a little carried away (likely on my end when the competitive juices started flowing). I remember one Saturday morning when my dad and I started bantering in the living room. My mom was working out in the guest room of our house, and my dad and I started a playful fight. Though playful, I obviously wanted to win. We ended up in the hallway as we danced away from the punches like Floyd Mayweather likes to do (that dude seems to run more than he punches, but he wins nonetheless). I pushed my dad against the wall, but this time was different than any time before. I pushed a little too hard and he ended up going through the wall by the bathroom.

3

Shocked, we both just looked at each other bewildered at what had just happened. We started to laugh nervously, and then my sweet momma walked in. I thought I was going to get in trouble, but to my surprise, my dad was the one who got the blame. This was one of the few instances that I actually got away with doing something wrong. *Marriage, am I right?*

But I've only been in one real fight in my life, and that was enough for me. I was 17 years old. It only lasted about 10 seconds and of course, it started with trash talk. It was early in the fall, school had just started, and I was away at the annual senior retreat. There was a group of about 10 senior boys in my cabin and we were about to leave for the afternoon activities. Somehow, as boys will be boys, a conversation began about who was the toughest and who could take on who. I would say I'm more of a lover than a fighter, so I wasn't too interested in the argument that was beginning to ensue. But then, I was slapped in the face and everything (my lover vs. fighter mentality) went out the window from there.

The fight began when I was slapped in the face. He hit part of my right ear and it began to ring. I was surprised he had slapped me instead of a punch and I reacted by punching him hard, as my right hand met his left jaw. And with that, the fight was over, and the respect was earned.

What I didn't mention to anyone else that day was that I could barely hear out of my right ear for the remainder of the day. Boy, was I relieved when I was back to normal the next morning.

While I am not much of fighter, I have always loved watching a good fight. War and boxing movies have always inspired me. One of my favorite underdog boxing stories starts with a man named Chuck from John Maxwell's book, *25 Ways to Win with People*...

An Underdog Story

Chuck Wepner was a boxer who was nicknamed the Bayonne Bleeder because of the physical beating he took while fighting. In the boxing world, he was known as a "catcher," a fighter who often uses his head to block the other guy's punches. Wepner continually pressured his opponent until he either won or got knocked out. He never cared how many shots he had to absorb before landing a knockout blow.

Trainer Al Braverman was quoted saying, "Wepner was the gutsiest fighter I ever met. He was in a league of his own. He didn't care about pain. If he got cut or elbowed, he never looked at me or the referee for help. He was a fighter in the purest sense of the word."

When Wepner knocked out Terry Henke in the 11th round in Salt Lake City, boxing promoter Don King offered him a title shot against the then heavyweight champion, George Foreman. But when Ali defeated Foreman, Wepner found himself scheduled to fight "the greatest," Muhammad Ali. On the morning of the fight, Wepner gave his wife a pink negligee and told her she would "soon be sleeping with the heavyweight champion of the world."

Ali scored a technical knockout with just 19 seconds remaining in the fight. But there was a moment—one glorious moment in the 9th round— when one single blow to Ali's chest knocked the reigning champion off his feet.

In that moment, Wepner recalled, "When Ali was down, I remember saying to my wingman, Al Braverman, 'Start the car, we're going to the bank, we're millionaires.'"

But to Wepner's surprise, Al responded, "You'd better turn around. Because he's getting up."

And after the fight was over and Ali had won, Wepner's wife pulled the negligee out of her purse and asked, "Do I go to Ali's room or does he come to mine?"

A struggling writer was watching this fight, and an idea came to him as he watched. He went home and wrote for three straight days. And that's how the birth of the Academy Award-winning movie Rocky came to life. A movie studio offered Sylvester Stallone $400,000 for his script, but he refused the money, choosing instead just $20,000 and the right to play the part of Rocky at $340 a week.

The movie studio also made Wepner an offer since the story was based on his life. He could receive a flat fee of $70,000 or 1% of the movie's gross profits. Wanting the guaranteed money, he took the $70,000, a decision that ultimately cost him $8 million. Today Chuck Wepner lives in Bayonne and works as a liquor salesman.

What you and I can learn from this story is this: **Who you are is the greatest asset you'll ever possess.** And as long as you recognize this valuable asset, accept it, increase it, and believe it—it will work like a charm.[1]

Am I Enough?

I think one of the top fears we will ever battle is found in our response to this question: *Am I enough?*

It can be far too easy to compare ourselves with other people. But there is a balance with comparison. "Comparison can be the thief of joy," like Theodore Roosevelt said, but it can also be a catalyst for growth. Comparison, like anything else, needs to be found in the middle at times. There can be too much and too little. At the end of the day, the standard we should hold ourselves to is found in being the best version of ourselves that we can be. We do this through the growth of our character from the standard found in God's Word.

As a teenager, I would often compare myself to the people around me. I was behaving well with above-average grades and not getting in near as much trouble as others. My parents quickly reminded me not to compare myself to other people, but to the Bible. This wise advice is a daily practice we have to remind ourselves of. The standard we focus on will be the growth that we see.

We all bring something to the table. There is room for all of us. The Apostle Paul writes about this in 1 Corinthians 12. He compares the church to a body. Just as a body has different parts and roles, so do we. How odd would it be if we all wanted to be placed in the same role as someone else and started walking around trying to use an eyeball as a leg? I can't help but think of Mike Wazowski from the Disney Pixar movie, *Monsters Inc.* That would be a peculiar looking bunch!

Some parts of the body may be more noticeable than others, but that does not mean they are more important. Paul talks more about this in verses 22-27:

"In fact, some parts of the body that seem weakest and least important are actually the most necessary. And the parts we regard as less honorable are those we clothe with the greatest care. So we carefully protect those parts that should not be seen, while the more honorable parts do not require this special care. So God has put the body together such that extra honor and care are given to those parts that have less dignity. This makes for harmony among the members, so that all the members care for each other. If one part suffers, all the parts suffer with it, and if one part is honored, all the parts are glad. All of you together are Christ's body, and each of you is a part of it."

So you see, there is room for all of us! You have a role and a voice. We need you, and we need you to be yourself. Be you because no one can do it better than you can. Other people will be a better version of them than you can be. On the flip side, no one can do what you can do. **When you recognize your value, you will turn on the value of your life.**

Relearning Confidence

Confidence is everything. Someone who is talented but lacks confidence won't do as much as the person who is less talented, but more confident. To be totally transparent with you, recognizing my value has been a struggle at times. It's a daily journey. There are times when I feel like the most confident person in the room and there are other times when I want to flee the scene. But that's what reminders are for. Too many times we forget to remember. Remembering is a crucial part of recognizing your value. I may have a long way to go, but I have come a long way. God isn't done with me yet. What He started, He will finish (1 Thessalonians 5:23-24).

I used to be really confident around the age of 20 when I had few responsibilities. People used to say I was too confident. I was arrogant at times, which began my journey of humility. I didn't want to be seen otherwise. Whenever I would have a cocky thought, I started to tell myself, "I'm nothing." After a while, I did

10

that enough that it worked. The opposite occurred though. I was much more humble, but I also lost sight of my value.

It seems like the older I get, the less I think of myself, which isn't necessarily a bad thing. But there definitely needs to be a balance. There is a confident humility that is available and required for success, maturity, and achievement.

A lot of times when we hear people say they are humble, we turn and say they are not. Can you be humble and also say you are? C.S. Lewis said, "Humility is not thinking less of yourself, but thinking of yourself less." My favorite example of this is found in Numbers 12:3 where the writer says, "Now Moses was more humble than any other person on earth." Guess who wrote Numbers? Moses! Yet, it's in the Bible and we believe it to be true. You can be humble and confident, and you can know it. It's a journey, but we can get there.

Believe in Yourself

A Philadelphia insurance executive who is a Civil War buff once closed a meeting by telling this story:

In the Civil War, Admiral David Farragut called Captain Samuel DuPont into his office to account for his failure to take his gunboats into Charleston Harbor.
Captain DuPont listed five reasons why he didn't make the raid.
Farragut replied, "Captain, there was another reason you have not mentioned."
"What is that?"
"You did not believe you could do it."[2]

How many times has the fear of failure gotten in the way of our faith for the future? We need to start focusing more on believing than doing. When you believe you can, you are normally right. Go for your dreams and your goals. Success starts by believing in yourself and embracing the value God created you with. If you did not have value, you would not have been created.

David leaves us with another gem in Psalm 8:5-6:

"For You made us only a little lower than God, and You crowned us with glory and honor. You put us in charge

of everything you made, giving us authority over all things."

When these verses were initially translated into the English language in the world-renowned King James Version, it had a major point missing. The translators put "angels" rather than "God." They wouldn't dare say we were a little lower than God, so they put lower than the angels. The original word David used is the name, "Elohim," which is one of the names used for God. It means strength and power.

The translators may have been intimidated to use the right translation. But false humility is not humility at all, and it's not what God intended for your life. When you follow Jesus, you carry His name and His power. We're in the family now. And there is tremendous value and confidence in knowing that.

The Heartbreakers

Levi Lusko once told a story about value that has always stuck with me. The story starts with a guy named Daryl who walked into a pawnshop in Los Angeles with a guitar. He opened the case and asked one of the workers what he could get for it. When the predictable bargaining was over, he walked out with a handful of cash. $250, to be precise. Not exactly winning the lottery. If the guitar had been left over from lessons he had taken as a child, that could even be considered decent money. But this was not some old guitar, and $250 was not close to market value. This guitar actually belonged to Tom Petty and was worth 80 times what Daryl sold it for. He ended up on the wrong side of this deal.

In addition to not being all that smart, Daryl was a thief. He worked as a security guard at a California soundstage, where Tom Petty and his world-famous Heartbreakers were rehearsing in preparation for a tour. One day the group discovered that 5 electric guitars were missing. Daryl was being paid to protect the gear in the facility, but it turned out that the gear actually needed protection from him. The 5 guitars he stole were worth more than $100,000 combined.

Perhaps Daryl was desperate for money, and so no price was too low. Or maybe he had an idea of what the instrument was actually worth. Though that would be hard to believe, considering who he stole it from. A quick Google search could have filled him in.

Like Levi Lusko says, **"When you don't know the value of what you have in your hands, you will always get from it far less than what it is worth."**[3]

Think Long

The most valuable company in the world as I write today is Apple. Three men cofounded this company in 1976 and Steve Jobs, who eventually became the chairman, CEO, and a legend to this day, is the most famous of the three. Most have heard of the second Co-Founder, Steve Wozniak, the genius who created the Apple I and Apple II computers. But chances are you haven't heard of the third member of the Apple trinity, Ronald Wayne. Wayne sketched the first logo, wrote the original partnership agreement, and created the first manual.

Ronald Wayne was a 10% shareholder in Apple. There are now 940 million active shares trading consistently above $500 per share. So that 10% stake would be worth at least $47 billion.[4]

However, less than 2 weeks after getting his 10% share, Ronald Wayne sold out for $800.

I think it's safe to say that by now you don't want to be like Ronald or Chuck.

When it comes to seeing your value and potential, you have to think long-term. Most of us overestimate what we can do in one year, but we underestimate what we can do in ten years. Life is a marathon, not a sprint. It's the ones who don't quit who win. Endurance is key to your development.

It may feel like no one is buying what you are selling at the moment but keep holding onto your value. Dita Von Teese says, "You can be a juicy ripe peach and there'll still be someone who doesn't like peaches." Not everyone will be a fan, but that doesn't mean you shouldn't be playing the game. People need what you have to offer. There were years that Apple was overlooked and unadmired, but here they are, decades later, outlasting and outperforming the crowd. Think long-term.

You Are Valuable

John Maxwell regularly tells a story of being on a speaking platform with his friend Gary Smalley when he did something that captivated the crowd. It goes a little something like this:

> *Before an audience of nearly ten thousand people, Gary held out a crisp fifty-dollar bill and asked them, "Who would like this fifty-dollar bill?" Hands started going up everywhere. "I am going to give this fifty-dollars to one of you," he said, "but first, let me do this." He*

16

proceeded to crumple up the bill. Then he asked, "Who still wants it?" The same hands went up in the air.

"Well," he continued, "what if I do this?" He dropped it on the ground and started to grind it into the floor with his shoe. He picked it up, all crumpled and dirty. "Now, who still wants it?" Again, hands went into the air.

"You have all learned a valuable lesson," Gary said. "No matter what I do to the money, you still want it because it doesn't decrease in value. It is still worth fifty dollars."

Many times, in our lives we are dropped, crumpled, and ground into the dirt by the decisions we make or the circumstances that come our way. We may feel as though we are worthless, insignificant in our own eyes and in the eyes of others. But no matter what has happened or what will happen, we never lose our value as human beings. Nothing can take that away. Never forget that.[5]

The point of the story is this: Recognize your value. When you recognize the value of your life, your life will become more valuable!

17

CHAPTER TWO

USE YOUR VOICE

"Find your voice and inspire others to find theirs."
- Stephen Covey

Losing your voice is one of those things that you don't plan for. It can be easy to take the five senses for granted. However, when we do lose one, we have to get creative in compensating for the loss.

One of my co-workers lost her voice recently. She happens to have a Keurig coffee maker in her office, so I wandered in one morning as I got to work. I like one cup in the morning and one cup in the afternoon. Jet black. If espresso is available, even better. A double espresso is my calling card.

Coffee preferences aside, I walked in on that Monday and said, "Good morning, how are you?" as I started to pop in the k-cup needed for my morning boost. When I didn't hear a response, I turned to see an unusual reaction.

She held up a small, white dry erase board and wrote, "I lost my voice this weekend. I have to use this for now." I told her I was sorry to hear that and walked away with my coffee.

The next day, we had our weekly staff meeting and there she was. Different day, same whiteboard. It was a little comedic, since I knew her voice would eventually return.

A couple of days later, I ran into her and she was beaming ear to ear. Her voice was back, and she was thrilled about it!

I'm so grateful I have a voice of my own. This small, seemingly irrelevant life event reminded me to be thankful for the voice I do have. We tend to take the little things for granted.

John Mayer

I have a few musical artists who I swear by. Everyone has a go-to when they get to pick the music. My four favorites over the past decade have been Coldplay, U2, Hillsong, and John Mayer. Recently, I've realized I'm becoming my father by the fact that I've been listening to talk radio or podcasts more than music nowadays. But let's not think on that. Cheers to adulting.

Back to John. I didn't care much for John Mayer in his early days of *Room for Squares*, *Heavier Things*, or even *Continuum*. (The fact that I included *Continuum* in that list feels sacrilegious.) I was with a friend in Best Buy one day and we walked by their home speaker department. They had John Mayer's "Where the Light Is" concert series playing on their big screen. The Dolby surround sound was serenading me, and I started to feel the magic. He played his cover of *Free Falling* by Tom Petty and The Heartbreakers and I thought to myself, Okay, this guy can sing. Then *Vultures* came on and I realized he could play guitar like a wizard. I bought his album that day and I was hooked.

Mayer quickly became my artist of choice over the next couple of years. Driving down the road with his albums playing in the car became an enjoyable routine for me. I can't sing a lick, so I would turn the volume up just loud enough where I could belt out the lyrics and still not hear myself.

iPad Only

While still on tour for his album, *Battle Studies*, Mayer began to work earnestly on his next project. However, around this time, he began to have vocal problems and sought medical assistance.

A granuloma was discovered on his vocal cords in 2011, showing damage caused by the growth. He began to search for treatments and had two surgeries. After trying multiple alternatives for a cure, they found Botox injections did the trick. But they also paralyzed his vocal cords for a while, placing him on a four-month vocal rest.

Four months is a long time to not be able to speak. This is especially long for one of the most famous musical artists of our time. He ended up moving from LA to a little town in Montana and used his iPad to talk and converse with people during this season.

Upon getting his voice back, Mayer said, "My dreams were in escrow, but when I found out this thing in my throat had receded, the most exciting thing for me was having a second chance at a new life. My dreams have come true twice. That's really cool."

Your Voice's Singularity

Most people have never lost their physical voice for an extended period of time. Many may not have the audience for their voice that John Mayer has. You may feel like your voice does not have the power to change the world. But a big part of changing the world is changing your world. Our nation is comprised of states. Our state is comprised of cities. Our cities have neighborhoods. Our neighborhoods have families. You have a family, and what builds strong cities and so on, are strong families.

We all have a voice, but there are many who have not discovered the power of their voice. Maybe you have not discovered the purpose of your voice. There is a singularity to your voice that no one else shares.

It's been said that we all have our own unique fingerprint. When you look at your fingertips closely, you may see the grooves, the lines, and the color that your finger provides. No one in the whole world has your exact fingerprint.

Studies have been done recently that say the same thing about your voice! No two voices are the same. Your voice is peculiar to you.

You have a voice. *What are you doing with it*?

Are you encouraging people or discouraging them?

Are you building people up or tearing them down?

Are you speaking in confidence or speechless in doubt?

Are you praying in faith or silent in fear?

God will use your voice if you open your mouth.

No one can make you talk. No one can make you write. You alone have the power to use your voice. If you do the best you can with your words, God will do what only He can do with the rest. God is a Creator and He works by using words first. When we speak, we are creating the future of our lives.

What are you doing with your voice?

Words that Matter

Hattie was born into one of the most distinguished families of pastors in America. Her father, Lyman Beecher, was considered to be one of the greatest speakers in America in 1850. That mantle was passed down to her brother, Henry, after their father passed away. But it was Hattie who would change the course of American history.

On a Sunday morning in 1851, during a communion service, Harriet fell into a trance similar to the trance that the Apostle Peter had on the rooftop of Simon the tanner's house. In her trance, Hattie saw an old slave being beaten to death. The vision left her so shaken that she could hardly keep from weeping. She walked her children home from church and skipped lunch. She immediately started writing down the vision God had given her, and words poured from her pen. When she ran out of paper, she found a brown grocery bag and continued to write. When she finally stopped and read what she had been writing for hours, she could hardly believe she had written it. It was nothing short of divine inspiration. Hattie said that God wrote the book—she just put the words on paper.

In January 1852, a year after Harriet Beecher Stowe's encounter, the vision was turned into a 45-chapter manuscript called *Uncle Tom's Cabin* and was prepared for publication. The publisher, John P. Jewett, didn't think the book would sell many copies. But over 3,000 were sold on the first day, and the entire first printing was sold out by the end of the second day. The third and fourth printings were sold out before the book was even reviewed. The book that Jewett didn't think would sell, ended up in almost every house in America—including the White House.

No novel has had a greater effect on the conscience of a country than Harriet Beecher Stowe's vision, Uncle Tom's Cabin. In fact, when Hattie met President Lincoln, he said, "So you're the little woman who started this Great War!" Never underestimate the power of a single prayer. Your voice matters![1]

Miracle Baby

My parents have been married for 44 years. I had to think about the math for a minute because it's hard to believe that's even possible. 44 years is a long time.

One of the struggles my parents went through, early on in their marriage, was not being able to have children. They prayed and waited on God, but this particular request wasn't answered for 12 long years.

At the time, there was a lady who worked with my parents at a thriving church called Word of Faith in the Dallas-Fort Worth area. This lady heard from God and felt like she was supposed to tell my mom, Bonnie, that she would become pregnant soon and would have a baby. That lady's name is Lisa Bevere.

Lisa was scared that saying something as bold as this to someone in her up-line might cause a stir, but she mustered up the strength, walked into my mom's office, and told her what she felt led to say. My mom took the words to heart and the conversation ended.

About a month later, I was conceived, and my mom was pregnant with me. I was born later that year on September 14, 1987. Though there were complications with the pregnancy, the baby they had believed and prayed for had arrived. Little did they know, that baby would have complications as well.

Hard of Hearing

I was born with Sensorineural Hearing Loss (SNHL). As I was growing up, I regularly had ear infections, which caused my temperature to rise very high. There were several occasions in my early years that I would have a temperature of 106-107 degrees. The doctors put tubes in my ears to help solve some of the problems.

By the time I turned two, I could only speak eight words (and they were fairly simple words at that). When you cannot hear well, you cannot speak well because you are unable to learn the language. When I was four years old, I had some advanced testing done at Children's Medical Hospital and they recommended that I take speech therapy classes, so I could converse like the kids my age. With that, I headed to the Collier Center in the Hospital District in Dallas where I took speech therapy classes for ten months.

My parents are people of faith, so they believed for God to heal me of my hearing loss. I talked with my mom this morning about this experience and she said,

"Dad and I are firm believers of this: You do everything you know to do, and then you let God do the rest."

During my time in speech therapy, my ears were retested, and the doctors found no evidence of hearing loss. My parents did what they could do, and then God did the rest.

From Therapy to Competitions

In first grade, I continued school at Lexington Academy. That year, we started doing verbal book reports. I quickly shifted from learning how to speak to learning how to speak in front of other people. I even got one of the leads in the Christmas play that year because I could speak so well and was comfortable on stage.

Over the next few years, my school would select people to represent our grade to compete in speech competitions with other schools. I went on to win awards and even won first place at one competition. Things were on the up and up.

Though my hearing and speech had developed greatly, it didn't change my personality. I'm naturally quiet and usually only speak up when I feel I can improve the silence or conversation being held. I would rather listen than talk, which is sometimes a great irony.

By the time middle school came around, I was at a new school. I dreaded having to do any kind of public presentation. Each time, my palms would become sweaty, my mouth would be dry, and my stomach would churn as I impatiently waited for my turn to go and speak in front of the class. It felt like a verse out of the Eminem song, Lose Yourself, "Knees weak, arms are heavy. There's vomit on his sweater already: Mom's spaghetti. He's nervous, but on the surface, he looks calm and ready."

Except on the surface, I didn't look calm and ready.

Middle school can be rough, so I can definitely identify with the reality of teenage emotions. I felt most comfortable out of the limelight. But that's not the destiny life had for me. Being comfortable isn't always the best thing for us. We aren't called to comfort ourselves, but we should help comfort others.

Speaking in Public

I became a Christian when I was 15 years old, and during the summer of 2005, before my senior year of high school, I felt like I was supposed to pursue becoming a pastor or a public speaker. I was excited about knowing what I wanted to do with the rest of my life, but I was also extremely nervous when the opportunity to speak actually came.

In August of 2005, I spoke a message for the very first time in front of about 100 people. I was trembling as I walked to the retreat cafeteria from my cabin where I would be doing the scheduled devotion after breakfast.

But despite my fear, that message went over much better than I could have ever dreamed. I felt a sense of purpose after I spoke and knew that my dreams of becoming a speaker were being confirmed. Teachers, coaches, and students would come up to me over the course of that year encouraging me to keep doing what I was doing.

Over the course of that year, I spoke about ten times at school chapels and events and started interning at Covenant Church with my youth pastor, Joel Scrivner, in the summer of 2006. I preached for the first time on September 9, 2006, at a Saturday night service. I still have the CD and I don't need to listen to it again to confirm that it was probably pretty awful.

Over the years, I began to develop the gift of speaking in public. Some messages were good, and some were not so good—but that's the beauty of development. Practice makes perfect. Or as Pastor Joel often says, practice makes confident.

Malcolm Gladwell speaks of a 10,000-hour rule that is required to gain expertise and confidence on any subject matter—and I couldn't agree with him more. I developed a good rhythm as I continued speaking, but I don't think I hit my groove until year ten of speaking. It takes hours upon hours of doing anything to gain the expertise and confidence you need to become successful. Slow and steady wins the race. Stick with it over the long haul and the results will come.

Here Come the Jitters

I started getting new exposure to adult audiences in the past few years, and I have had to relearn some of the confidence and comfort I had while speaking to teenagers. But the more opportunity I got, the more I had to deal with the jitters and nerves again.

I would question whether I was good enough, as a person and as a communicator. I questioned whether I looked the part and if people noticed my limp more than my words (more on this in *Desirable Difficulties).*

It has been a process, but ultimately, it has led me to recognize my value. Either I am God's idea, or I am not. Either I have a purpose, or I do not. I have chosen to believe the positive. And there are several examples and stories of others battling their own insecurities that have provided encouragement for me along the way.

Moses' Stutter

One of the greatest leaders in human history was a Bible character named Moses.

When Moses was eighty years old, God appeared to him and called him to deliver His people, the Israelites, from slavery in Egypt. But Moses kept providing excuse after excuse as to why he wasn't the right man for the job. He would say things like, "Who am I? Who will I say sent me? They won't believe me," and then he landed with this in Exodus 4:10-12:

But Moses pleaded with the Lord, "O Lord, I'm just not a good speaker. I never have been, and I'm not now, even after you have spoken to me. I'm clumsy with words."

And God quickly answered him saying,

we always tell ourselves we're not good enough for what he has planned, but God says we are

32

"Who makes mouths? Who makes people so they can speak or not speak, hear or not hear, see or not see? Is it not I, the Lord? Now go, and do as I have told you. I will help you speak well, and I will tell you what to say."

Who makes mouths? What a response. Moses tried to make another excuse, but God didn't budge and sent Moses' brother, Aaron, with him. They went to Egypt, and the rest is history.

If we only go by what Moses said, we would believe that he had a stutter or that he was a poor speaker. We tend to forget that the most powerful family and father in the world adopted Moses at that time. He grew up in the Pharaoh's household in Egypt. He was raised as a prince. He received the best of everything for forty years.

In Acts 7:22, this is recorded of Moses:

*"Moses was taught all the wisdom of the Egyptians, and he became mighty in both **speech** and action."*

Wait, *what?* Everyone considered Moses to be a mighty speaker and a powerful man of action. Yet, Moses looked at himself as a poor speaker and a man who needed all the help he could get to accomplish what God asked of him.

Moses had forgotten the power of his voice. After years of choosing to have a passive voice, he ended up having passive action. But then God came along and spoke life to the brokenness inside of him, and the rest is history.

Isn't that just like us?

Our gifts and talents may be obvious to other people, but when we look at ourselves in the mirror, we see someone totally different. The key is to see yourself as God sees you. When Moses said, "I'm not," God said, "I Am."

And God is saying the same to you.

God sees you like he does so see yourself like he does.

Monologues Over Ping-Pong

I'll never forget the night I lost 10 straight games of ping-pong. Nothing crazy happened per se, but I did learn a very valuable lesson.

I had gone with Pastor Joel to a service at a conference he was speaking at. We ended the night by getting some late-night takeout and stopping by the Neo (our old youth building) to play some Ping-Pong. I routinely beat all of my opponents at Ping-Pong, but I couldn't seem to meet my match with Joel Scrivner.

It was nearing 10 p.m., I had lost several games, and I was hungry for a win. (If you play against me in something, I will typically want to keep playing until I win. That may take five minutes or three hours—the choice is yours.) We were in game six and I had finally taken an advantage. We were going to 15 and I was ahead 11-5, sure that I was finally going to beat my sensei.

It was at this moment that Joel started talking to himself out loud. I looked across the table and heard him say, "C'mon Joel. You're better than this. Play to your full potential. Let's win this. You're a champ!"

I was a little perplexed and started to chuckle. But the joke was on me. Joel ended the game going on a 10-1 run and handed me the loss. I thought to myself, *This has got to be one of the reasons he is a four-time World Champion in taekwondo. He literally talked himself into winning.*

The Power of Self-Talk

There is power in self-talk. I've watched how this works (and doesn't work) in others' lives and now I swear by practicing it daily in my own life too.

For 15 years now, I have made it a habit to confess the right things out loud. It is not enough to just believe or think something. You have to say it.

Your mind has to follow your mouth.

Say this out loud: *Pink elephant.*

No, really, say it.

Pink elephant.

What are you thinking of? I would bet—a pink elephant.

Let's try this again.

Say this word out loud: *Tomato.*

What are you thinking of? I would put money on the fact that you're thinking of tomatoes (and maybe, your love or hate for them).

The point is this: Your mind will always follow what your voice is saying. It works every single time. If you are not thinking the right things, maybe you should start saying the right things.

1. Use your voice to beat temptation.

There are three things I want to point out about self-talk, and the first is found in Matthew Chapter 4 with a story about how Jesus started His ministry. At this time, Jesus had been fasting everything but water for forty days—and He was tired and hungry. That is a dangerous combination. The devil showed up and tempted Jesus in three ways by asking Jesus, *"Are you who God says you are? Will God do what He said He would do? Is God who He says He is?"*

Each time Jesus was tempted, He would use His voice to quote a verse of scripture. And each time, he overcame temptation.

If Jesus has to use the Bible to defeat temptation, so do you.

This is something I have learned to practice for years. When I was twenty, I found a page of verses on anger in one of my drawers. I had forgotten that I used to have an issue with anger until I found that paper with verses on it and recognized how much the Word of God had changed my heart and mind. The title at the top was, "My Confessions of Who I am in Christ."

Nowadays, when I am tempted, I can pull out my phone, head to the notes section, and mutter a verse that is related to what I am going through. This immediately changes my mindset and outlook on the problem at hand. But here's the catch: You have to know the Word to quote the Word. If I'm going to be a man of my word, I have to be a man of the Word. If I'm going to read the Bible, I have to let the Bible read me.

2. Use your voice to overcome fear.

This has been the number one way I have learned to use God's Word. But the same practice works for every situation we can encounter in life. If I'm dealing with anything, there is a verse for that.

In 2 Timothy 1:6, Paul tells Timothy, "God has not given you a spirit of fear, but of power, love, and a sound mind." I have to remind myself of that. We all do. The enemy knows that he cannot stop you, so he is doing everything he can to intimidate you.

Paul even addresses his fear in Acts 18:9-10. You'll never see Paul talking about his fear up to this point. But just because you don't address it, doesn't mean it's not addressing you. Just because you're not talking about it does not mean it is not talking about you. Jesus didn't tell Paul to just get over it. He gave Paul the remedy for fear in Acts 18:9: "Keep on speaking. I am with you."

You don't think your way out of fear. You talk your way out of fear.

Whenever I feel fear, I start to feel suffocated in a way. Fear is like a python that wants to choke the life out of you. The only way to overcome fear is to talk yourself out of it. Use your voice and start declaring the

Word of God! Don't just say it once. Keep saying it and keep moving.

One of my favorite verses of the past couple of years is found in 2 Samuel 23:2. It is included as part of King David's last words. He said, "The Spirit of the Lord speaks through me. His words are upon my lips." I love that. Whenever I feel like I don't have something valuable to say or need to gather more confidence, I just remind myself of that truth.

One of the powerful things about God's Word is that it may have been initially spoken to someone else, but it can still apply to you. God's Word does not return void (Isaiah 55:11). It just keeps on working and it is meant for you to use also.

3. Use your voice to find your voice.

You will never find your rhythm or style until you just start speaking. The singularity of your voice will be found when you keep using your voice. But the most powerful tool we have is learning to say and agree with what God says about you.

To this day, I have three pieces of paper with about thirty verses on them that I will speak out loud over myself in the privacy of my room. When I speak His Word, it reminds me of who I am and Whose I am.

Doing this has changed my attitude and lifted my self-esteem over days, weeks, and months. It is one of the best practices I have in my personal life.

God wants to speak through you. It may not be on a stage, but He will speak in and through your life if you let Him. But it's the same thing, honestly—whether you speak on stage or through your life. Just speak out for Him in all you say and do.

There is a statement I used to love by Francis of Assisi, but I have conflicting feelings about it now. "Preach Jesus, and if necessary, use words." I think some of us like that because we're scared to speak out and are delighted by the fact that we can do so by being silent. Your life speaks, but your voice speaks as well. I believe you need both.

Madeleine Albright said, "It took me quite a long time to develop a voice, and now that I have it, I am not going to be silent."

Be bold, and let God speak through you. God will use your voice if you open your mouth.

PART II

WHAT
ARE YOU
MADE OF?

CHAPTER THREE

YOU CAN'T TEACH DESIRE

"Our Lord finds our desires not too strong, but too weak. We are half-hearted creatures, fooling about with drink and sex and ambition when infinite joy is offered us."
- C.S. Lewis

Have you ever *really* wanted something? Of course, you have. But wanting, more often than not, requires money. And, I've found that people tend to either be spenders or savers. What's ironic is when two people get married and you have one of each trying to live in a unified partnership. Now that is some dynamic tension.

I don't want to cause any tension right now though. I just want you to think about when you really wanted something. When you just *had* to have it. Everyone has moments when they see something they want. It could be a purse, a car, a pair of jeans or shoes. You might have twenty pairs of shoes laying on your closet floor, but your focus will be on the ones you really want, right now. We don't want to admit it and it sounds silly when you say it out loud, but it happens to the best of us. Everyone has their eye on something.

I'm Back

The year was 1995. Michael Jordan was in his first year of retirement from the game of basketball, but speculation started to heat up that he was eyeing a return to the Chicago Bulls.

On Friday, March 17, Chicago radio stations reported that the deal was done—Jordan would soon make his announcement that he would play on the upcoming Sunday in a nationally televised game against Indiana. While waiting for the announcement to take place, fans kept a close watch at the Jordan statue outside the United Center, which had quickly become somewhat of a shrine. Over at the Berto Center, a growing crowd of fans and media milled about, with some fans leaning from the balconies of the Residence Inn next door. Everyone was waiting for the official word.

Suddenly, practice was over, and Jordan's Corvette appeared on the roadway. With the fans cheering wildly, he gunned the engine and sped off.

Next came Scottie Pippen in a Range Rover, pausing long enough to flash a giant smile through the vehicle's darkly tinted windows. Moments later, Peter Vecsey did a stand-up report outside with the fans rooting in the background. He told the broadcast audience that Michael Jordan was returning, that he would play against Indiana on Sunday, and that he would probably pull his old number 23 jersey out of retirement. Excitement coursed through the city. Later that day, the star of stars broke his silence with a two-word press release, issued through his agent. It read, "I'm back."[1]

Shoe Game

The Bulls, back in the 1995 playoffs, faced the young Orlando Magic. The Magic had a tandem of young stars named Shaquille O'Neal and Anfernee "Penny" Hardaway. The Bulls ended up losing this series before going on their 3-peat as NBA Champions the next three years. Two important things happened in this series though. Jordan brought his number 23 jersey out of retirement in the second game after hearing an opposing teammate mock the new 45 number he had been wearing. Nick Anderson trash talked MJ after game one saying, "Number 45 is not number 23." Say no more fam.

Jordan also debuted his most iconic shoe in this game, the Air Jordan XI. He wore the "Concord 11's" for two games in the series and was fined $5,000 each game for not wearing a solid black shoe like the rest of the team. This only added to the legend.

Jordan ended up releasing these shoes in November of 1995 and anyone that watched basketball wanted to cop a pair. Including me.

I was eight years old when the Jordan 11's came out. My best friend and I both wanted these coveted shoes. Christmas was just around the corner and I excitedly made my Christmas List with the shoes right at the top. I went to the room in our home where we had a 1992 PC with the new 1995 Word. (Can we just take a moment to thank God that technology has come a long way since then?)

Computers were not much to look at back in the day, but then again, I didn't know what the future would hold in light of technology to come. I just knew I wanted a Game Boy with *Donkey Kong* on it, the Jordan 11's, and a VHS copy of Disney's *Lion King*. Remember the way the case would crack open as you got ready to pop that movie into the VCR? The *Lion King* was the first movie that *almost* made me cry. Well, let's be honest, I did cry.

When Christmas rolled around, I got the other presents I had asked for, but no Jordan 11's were under the tree. I had probably expected too much, but I was disappointed nonetheless. I reached over to my home phone attached with a cord and dialed up my friend to see if he had received a pair. He had, and I had not.

A few months passed, and I had forgotten about the shoes. But then in 2000, they had a re-release. Same story, same results.

Fast-forward fifteen years to 2015. I started thinking about the shoes again. Normally, I will think about something and the thought will pass, but after a couple of months, I decided to go ahead and act on my impulse. I'm normally very frugal, but my wife is helping to expand my taste. My friend, Cassius, told me about a website in China where I could find Jordan's for less than $100. The catch was this: they were fake. Let me stop here and say, no one has saved me more money in my life than my dad and Cassius. So, I went for it and bought the Jordan 11's. I waited a month for them to arrive. But the package finally came and the moment I had been waiting years for was here. I sat down, laced up my new Jordan's, looked in the mirror and thought to myself, *That's it?* After years of waiting, I was expecting a more fulfilled feeling.

But the problem was, I had hyped up the purchase over time and didn't even get the real thing. A couple of years passed, and I ended up buying the authentic Jordan's. This time, I had a much different reaction and yelled out in excitement. These were the shoes I had been waiting for.

Real recognizes real. Real is better than artificial. A real burger is better than a turkey burger. Chicken is better than tofu. Chocolate is better than sugar-free. Rolex is better than Folex. Jordan's are better than Nordans. Wait for the real thing!

Can I Have Your Number?

Have you ever wanted *someone*? Let's face it, when we develop a crush on someone, we will do whatever it takes to get noticed by them. You might like a picture of theirs on social media. One of the best ways is to find a mutual friend and get them working on your behalf. You might send a DM. You may put yourself in their environment more often to improve your odds of being recognized and developing a relationship before you make a move.

When I started hanging out with my now wife as friends, it wasn't long before I started liking her as more than a friend. She was a person that I just had to be in a relationship with. It's said that a spouse is not someone you could live with, but someone you would not want to live without. When you have a desire to know or be with someone, you will go to extraordinary lengths to get what you want.

Desire is the Fire

We desire some things and some people in a way that we will do anything to get them. When are we going to be a generation who desires God like that?

We have heard words, dreams, and visions about what this generation can do. But when are we going to *do* it? Dreams and plans for the future are fine. But do it! Don't tell me what you're going to do in the future. Get started, and start doing it now.

The best people and leaders have not been the ones who over-promise and under deliver. They have been the ones who under-promise and over deliver. They just keep showing up with a great attitude, loving Jesus, and loving people. They have desire!

Desire is the fire. One of the frustrating things in life is that you can't teach people desire.

You can teach leadership.

You can teach history.

You can teach on attitude.

You can teach about marriage.

You can teach a language.

You can teach about winning with people.

You can teach about religion.

You can teach about fitness.

But you can't teach desire.

Some people have the heart to do something, and some people don't. You can teach someone the skill, but you can't teach desire.

Showtime Lakers

Pat Riley is one of the great coaches in NBA History, but it didn't start out like that. Riley was hired at age thirty-six to coach the Los Angeles Lakers, who had already been led to one championship by Magic Johnson. He had played in the NBA as an average journeyman player and he got the job with the Lakers as an interim coach, but they were looking for a different coach.

Pat became known as the NBA's most demanding coach, but also as one of its best motivators. He had a Hollywood style and walked the sidelines with slicked-back hair, Armani suits, and a cool confidence. The Lakers reached seven NBA Finals in Pat Riley's first eight years. They became known as the "Showtime" Lakers and were led by their fearless head coach. Magic Johnson, Kareem Abdul-Jabbar, and James Worthy played their way to the Hall of Fame on the court. This group of Lakers is known to be one of the best NBA teams of all time. But at times, even they struggled with desire.

One game, in particular, stands out. The Lakers were playing in the Finals against the mighty Boston Celtics. They were down in the series and needed the win, but they showed up flat with no energy. Down by 20 at the half, the Lakers slumped to the locker room and took a seat. As they sat disengaged, Pat Riley walked over to a big Gatorade jug of ice water and completely submerged his head inside. A few were startled at first, but it took about thirty seconds for all the players to look up in curiosity. One minute passed and the curiosity turned to concern as the team stood to surround their coach. At the 2:30 mark they struggled to pull their coach up out of the water and around 3 minutes, Riley finally pulled his head out, gasping for air. His hair was wet, eyes were red, and his face was pink from the cold.

Completely out of breath, he asked them, "When are you going to want to win like I just wanted to breathe?"

The Lakers ended up winning that game by 15 points. Turns out, they won the series as well. The message was clear. They had to have the desire to win. Desire is the fire.

Hot and Cold

About 2,000 years ago, Jesus gave His disciple John, a message for seven churches. One of them was delivered to the Church of Laodicea. In the message recorded in Revelation 3:15-22, He says this:

"I know all the things you do, that you are neither hot nor cold. I wish that you were one or the other! But since you are like lukewarm water, neither hot nor cold, I will spit you out of my mouth! You say, 'I am rich. I have everything I want. I don't need a thing!' And you don't realize that you are wretched and miserable and poor and blind and naked. So I advise you to buy gold from me—gold that has been purified by fire. Then you will be rich. Also buy white garments from me so you will not be shamed by your nakedness, and ointment for your eyes so you will be able to see. I correct and discipline everyone I love. So be diligent and turn from your indifference. Look! I stand at the door and knock.

If you hear my voice and open the door, I will come in,
and we will share a meal together as friends. Those
who are victorious will sit with me on my throne, just as
I was victorious and sat with my Father on his throne.
Anyone with ears to hear must listen to the Spirit and
understand what he is saying to the churches."

In this passage, we clearly see a group of people that are stuck in the middle.

The city of Laodicea was in between two cities, Hierapolis and Colossae. Hierapolis was known for its natural hot springs and people would come from great distances to get in these ancient saunas. They viewed it as a medicinal and therapeutic practice that could improve their health. People also traveled to Colossae where they had ice-cold water. They invigorated themselves by taking frequent dips into the famous, refreshing, cool-to-freezing waters of the city.

Laodicea was the biggest and richest city, but it did not have hot or cold water. In a desire to get hot water for themselves, a huge construction project commenced, and they built a six-mile pipeline from Hierapolis to Laodicea—a real feat at the time! However, the water lost its heat along the way. By the time it arrived, it was lukewarm and developed a sickening, nauseating taste. No one would drink it. They spit it out!

Jesus looked at the people in the church of Laodicea and said, "You are like that."

So, what are you? Hot, cold, or lukewarm? What are we as a Christian church? This isn't condemning news. This should simply encourage us to move in the right direction.

Jesus said in verse 19, "Be diligent and turn from your indifference." All repentance is, is turning from the wrong thing to the right One.

We've all been in a bath that started hot and then slowly turns lukewarm and cold. The challenge for us is to stay hot. If we provide the oil, Jesus will provide the fire. If we provide availability, Jesus will provide the anointing.

The great revivalist, Smith Wigglesworth said, "God will choose availability over anointing every day." He is the one who anoints, but He won't make you available. That's our job.

Draw Near

One of my favorite verses in the Bible is written by James, the brother of Jesus. Before we look at it, I want to ask you this: *What would it take for you to believe that your brother or sister was God?* That would be a hard truth to swallow! Here is a person who sleeps in my house, appears pretty normal most of the time, received my hand-me-down clothes growing up—and now they're saying that they are God. For me to believe that, I would need some pretty strong evidence of them living a perfect, sinless life. Maybe even dying and being raised to life afterward. James had the same reaction. He was not a believer, but after seeing all of this happen before his eyes, He realized that this was the Savior of the world.

James wrote a book, which he aptly called, *James.* That makes it easy when it comes to book titles, I guess. In Chapter 4:8 he states, "Draw near to God, and He will draw near to you."

Who draws first? You do. When I take a step toward God, He takes a step toward me. When I desire God, He desires me. Here's what is so wild about that. When I have a bad day or decide to run away from God in certain areas of life, does He draw away from me? No. He stays right where He is. Evidence even suggests that He doesn't just stay there, but actually pursues us and desires us even when we don't desire Him.

If I keep drawing near to God, He will keep

drawing near to me. When I keep doing that, I will have a close relationship with Him. You cannot keep walking toward someone and not end up side by side or face to face with them. This concept paints the same picture for us.

If we are going to change our world, it starts with desire. It starts with taking a step toward God.

Thirsty?

King David is known for many things. The book he helped pen, *Psalms*, is one of his most noteworthy accomplishments in life. He bares his soul throughout most of it and we can identify with the emotions David displays. He had high highs and he had low lows. Yet despite his faults and grievous sins, God speaks of David after his life was over, saying, "David is a man after God's own heart."

How can a man with such serious errors be called that? I believe one of the reasons is because each time he sinned and missed the mark, he drew nearer to God. He always ended up in repentance and coming back to God.

There is a passage that has stayed with me for years now that has described David's desire for God. He writes in Psalms 42:1-2, "As the deer pants for streams of water, so I long for you, O God. I thirst for God, the living God. When can I come and stand before him?"

The word for deer in this passage actually describes a type of deer called a hart. Harts were known to live in the dry, arid wilderness where there was not much water to be found. On the rare days, a hart would find a stream of water, it would gulp as much water as possible to get hydrated and quench its thirst. As soon as it drank, it would start to walk away. But before long, the hart would turn around and go back to the river of water to get another drink, not knowing when the next drink would come.

David looks at the hart, and writes to God, "As the hart pants for water, so I long for you, God!"

David had a heart for God. He had a desire for life and for people. Desire is the fire.

There is a quote from D.L. Moody that has always stayed with me. He said, "If you set yourself on fire for God, people will come and watch you burn."

I wonder if you will make that decision for God today. Maybe you have made it before. Maybe this is the first time. But you can either say, "one day" or "day one." You decide.

This is something I have to daily remind myself

of. We have to consciously make the decision to live a life that is hot. If we don't focus on our desire for God, we will become stagnant. Our heart's desire must be this: *God, I want to know you. Use me however you want. Give me the desire to love you and love your people. I'm available. As the deer pants for water, so I long for you, God.*

If you are filled with desire, people will come and join you. Likeminded people always come alongside you in life. When you live a life full of desire, passionate people living a purposeful life will surround you! Desire is the fire of life.

CHAPTER FOUR

STAND FIRM

"Be sure you put your feet in the right place, then stand firm."
- Abraham Lincoln

I am going to start this chapter off by saying, "I have the world's best parents." I'll continue that notion by saying, growing up, I thought I had the world's most *strict* parents. (I laugh at that thought now as I remember my teenage years.)

When it came to movies, nothing was allowed in our home except PG or G ratings. I felt robbed! The only way around that rule was to wait nearly two years for the movies I wanted to watch to come out on TV and then pray that I would be allowed to watch it then when the foul language had been dubbed over. Garbage in, garbage out was the mantra.

It didn't get any easier when it came to music. All my friends were listening to Eminem, Britney Spears, Backstreet Boys, Nickelback (we knock them now, but everyone loved them back then), the All-American Rejects, Destiny's Child, Justin Timberlake, and more. I was able to listen to Creed (remember them?) and some U2 songs, but that was about it. Thank God for DC Talk and Delirious, but those are the only Christian bands I'll name here. Long live CCM (Contemporary Christian Music).

The year was 2002 and the movie that everyone was seeing was *Mr. Deeds*, starring the incomparable Adam Sandler. If you only know Adam Sandler from recent movies, trust me when I say his movies were much more entertaining fifteen years ago in his prime. He brought us *Happy Gilmore*, *The Waterboy*, *Big Daddy*, and then, in June 2002, *Mr. Deeds*.

Looking back, I don't think I would have missed much by not seeing this movie, but peer pressure is alive and well in every generation—especially as a young person.

My best friend from the neighborhood insisted we go see this movie. Everyone in school had seen it, and it was too hot outside to keep playing hoops in the front yard. My parents were at work and expected me to stay at my friend's house all day, so I said, "Yeah, of course! Let's go see it!" knowing this would be the perfect time to go.

We ended up buying tickets for the movie at a local theater later that afternoon, but toward the end of the movie, my Nokia cell phone started to buzz in my pocket. It was my mom. Then, my dad. I instantly felt dread as I knew I had left the house without their permission to watch a movie they wouldn't have liked me to see.

Growing up with Christian parents can be interesting. It's a known fact that Christian moms will tell their children, "Jesus will tell me if you're up to no good!" That statement would put the fear of God in us because, somehow, it seemed to be true. Momma's always find out!

I quickly left the theater, answered the phone, and told them the truth. I knew I was going to "the sunken place" after that call. And I was right. I ended up getting grounded, but I learned a valuable lesson that day.

It can be hard to stand firm and do what you know is right, especially when you want to do what is wrong. I don't have a problem with that movie. The problem was found in me being deceitful and not honoring my parents. I would soon get better at standing firm, but not quite yet.

Have you ever had to stand up for a long time? Maybe it was in a long line or waiting for a roller coaster at Six Flags. One of the things they don't tell you before you get married is about how uncomfortable it can be to stand in one place during the wedding ceremony. Standing in one place for a long time trying to have good posture can be painful. My legs, ankles, and feet were on fire. I was about to whisper and say, "Hurry up, Pastor!" But thankfully, I kept my cool. It can be hard to stand firm, physically and spiritually.

Too Close for Comfort

One of the stories that has taught me the most about standing firm comes from a single day in Moses' life. We find the story in Exodus 17:8-16:

"While the people of Israel were still at Rephidim, the warriors of Amalek attacked them. Moses commanded Joshua, 'Choose some men to go out and fight the army of Amalek for us. Tomorrow, I will stand at the top of the hill, holding the staff of God in my hand.' So Joshua did what Moses had commanded and fought the army of Amalek. Meanwhile, Moses, Aaron, and Hur climbed to the top of a nearby hill. As long as Moses held up the staff in his hand, the Israelites had

the advantage. But whenever he dropped his hand, the Amalekites gained the advantage. Moses' arms soon became so tired he could no longer hold them up. So Aaron and Hur found a stone for him to sit on. Then they stood on each side of Moses, holding up his hands. So his hands held steady until sunset. As a result, Joshua overwhelmed the army of Amalek in battle. After the victory, the Lord instructed Moses, 'Write this down on a scroll as a permanent reminder, and read it aloud to Joshua: I will erase the memory of Amalek from under heaven.' Moses built an altar there and named it Yahweh-Nissi (which means "the Lord is my banner"). He said, 'They have raised their fist against the Lord's throne, so now the Lord will be at war with Amalek generation after generation.'"

There are a handful of notes I took away from reading this passage on standing firm and how it relates to us today. Notice it records that the warriors of Amalek came to fight against them. One translation even says that they "sought occasion" to fight, meaning they were looking for a fight. We have all come across certain people in our lives who are just looking for a fight. We might be wearing a smile and even open the door for them, but they are looking for any reason to argue and fight. That is what Amalek is doing. The Amalekites were descendants of a man named Esau. The group of people Moses was leading, the Israelites, were descendants of a man named Jacob. Esau and Jacob were brothers.

These people are family members.

These people are cousins.

These people are old friends.

Familiar people will try to get you to compromise.

The people who know us the best and see us the most are oftentimes the people who are most familiar with us. As you may know by now, most people don't like change. Change is uncomfortable. There may come a time in your life when you decide to stand firm in your convictions, your values, and who you know you are called to be. We expect in our optimism that everyone will be excited and happy for us when we change for the better. The opposite can happen fairly often though. You will have old friends, and maybe even family members, who try to get you to compromise the ground you've taken as you seek to improve your life and live by your Christian values.

Sometimes, the people you have the most history with have the hardest time seeing you change for the best. People will either be inspired by your leadership and change with you or feel defensive because of their own insecurities and shortcomings. Don't take it personally. People are going to do what they want to do, but all you are responsible for is yourself. That's it. You won't answer for what other people do with their lives. All you will answer for is what you chose to do with your life. Most people just want things to remain the same, but you are better than that.

Defining Moment

When I was 15 years old, I made the decision to follow Jesus personally. It was a defining moment in my life. I wasn't at church. No one led an altar call. In fact, I had just had a heated argument with my dad in our living room. I had the gall to ask him, *"Are you done?!"* You know what happened after. He was *not* done. He handled it really well, as I look back at that moment. I would have whooped my tail, but he just said he was not done and continued to correct me for a few minutes after. When the conversation ended, I stormed out of the room (God bless you if you are a parent of a teenager) and met eyes with a picture we had hanging on the wall in our hallway.

You know how people will have family pictures, artwork, or décor hanging in the halls of their homes? After the newness wears off, we rarely even notice what is hanging there anymore. It just becomes part of the house. But for whatever reason, on this night, I noticed a picture of an older couple that had babysat me while I was growing up. Their names are Gene and JoAnne Brinson. What a couple. JoAnne babysat kids out of her home for thirty-some years or more. They even declared a "JoAnne Brinson Day" in her hometown of Carrollton, Texas in 1983. She made a massive impact in her community.

I looked right into Mrs. JoAnne's eyes as I stormed out and broke. You see, JoAnne had passed away from Lou Gehrig's disease two years prior. Before she had passed, whenever I would go to her house, she would always tell me the same four words as she hugged and kissed me on the cheek. She would lean over, look me in the eyes and affirm me by saying, "Jesus loves you, Brandon." It was something I heard a lot growing up in a Christian home, and honestly—I took it for granted. It was just something she said. But that night, I looked her in the eyes, and I remembered her words. *Jesus loves me.*

Paul wrote to the Romans and told them that it is the loving-kindness of God that leads us to repentance (Romans 2:4). That night, I was overwhelmed by the goodness of God and His kindness toward me. I walked outside to sit on the driveway and prayed as I looked up to the sky. My prayer was simple, but it was sincere. All I said was, "God, I'm done doing it my way. I want to do things your way. Jesus, I am following You. You are the Lord of my life." And my life was forever changed.

Histories and Futures

Fast-forward a few months, and I was hanging out with one of my friends in his neighborhood. I realized we were in the same neighborhood as one of my elementary crushes. I had a history with this girl, so I decided to knock on her door to see if she still lived there. (Boys will be boys, *right*?) I knocked confidently, and there she was. She was still beautiful, and the familiar sparks began to fly. We started dating some after that. I will say, I technically wasn't allowed to date at this time. (I might have been a Christian at this point, but I was still sixteen.)

Long story short, this girl ended up being my first kiss. I remember feeling convicted by it and knowing this was an important time for me. I felt I needed to separate myself and not date anyone for a while. I remember telling her via AIM. (For those of you not old enough to remember, that stands for AOL Instant Messenger and it would be like breaking up with someone via text these days.) Mature, I know.

Writing this story down just brought me back. I'm not going to tell you my username—okay, it was SilkySmooth80. *Man, I needed Jesus.* Thank God I upgraded to Legendary705 after that.

Back to the story. I broke things off with her and I could tell she was surprised, but she respected my decision. We both went our own separate ways, and I ended up not dating at all for the rest of high school.

Wise decision, I would say. I believe this choice really helped my growth in my formative years of becoming a godly, young man.

But this year, I heard the news that this particular girl had a tragic series of events in her life. She had overdosed on drugs and passed away. My heart sank when I heard the news and my prayers went out for her family. She had her struggles and addictions over the years, and it appeared that she had never course corrected her life.

I learned a valuable lesson from this turn of events: **Just because you have a history with someone doesn't mean you have a future with them.**

History does not equal future. Just because you have been friends with someone in the past does not mean they have earned the right to be in your future.

Go with people you can grow together with.

Be bold and stand firm in your convictions.

Be more mindful of your future than your history when making decisions.

Joshua's Turn

Back to Moses. In Exodus 17, verses nine and ten, a young man named Joshua was mentioned. Some people will say, "Well, of course, Joshua would step up to the plate," because we know some forty-years later, Joshua would assume leadership of the Israelite nation after Moses and become the leader of 1-2 million people in a day.

But this verse was the very first time he was ever mentioned in scripture. **There is a first time to stand firm for everyone.**

There are people in your life that you respect and admire. You may think they are the strongest people in your life. They may be bold and confident.

They would never compromise. But did you know, there was a first time for them? There was a first time to stand firm for every single person you look up to. That time was followed by another time. Maybe they messed up a few times and fell short. But they got back up and stood firm again.

The wisest man to ever live, King Solomon, had this to say about such people: "The righteous may trip seven times, but each time they will rise again" (Proverbs 24:16). That word, "seven," actually refers to many. The righteous may fall many times, but each time they get back up. Notice, we are known by how we get back up, not by how we fall down. The key is getting up.

The toughest time to stand your ground can be early on in life. If you don't do it then, maybe you never will. The time is now to start. *If not now, when?*

Summer Momentum

I had a pivotal summer before my senior year of high school. I went all-in that summer concerning my relationship with God, in my love for people, and my preparation for who I wanted to be. My theme for that summer was: *The time is now. Now is the time.* It was a defining summer for me. It preceded a senior year where I would start speaking and preaching publicly. It was the year when I got connected to my future mentor and leader.

The longer you stand firm, the easier it will get. The more you do something, the better you will do it and the more confident you will become.

The next thing I noticed about Moses in Exodus 17 is found in verses nine and eleven. I always thought that Moses holding the staff up was some quirky thing that God told him to do. But as I read this story again, God never told Moses to hold his staff up. God never said a word about it.

Sometimes, you don't need to pray. You need to act. Lead by example. Moses was the leader, so he set the example. He was basically saying, "When you need leadership or encouragement, just look at me. I will be holding my staff up letting you know to fight well! The Lord is for us and we will win!"

Your influence will influence those around you to fight or flee.

If you are reading this, you are a leader. Leadership is influence. You may be a leader at home, at work, in your community, at school, online, at church, or somewhere else. But if someone is looking up to you, then you are leading them. If they are imitating your actions, then lead well.

If you want to become a better leader, then find good leaders to follow. Spend time with them, read their books, get a mentor, and start displaying good leadership qualities yourself. Leadership is not always about talking—it's more about doing. Leadership has nothing to do with popular opinion. Leaders go the way and show the way. We lead by example.

Won't My Arms Get Tired?

My favorite part of this story is next. It says that Moses' arms got tired. I can only imagine. But then, two people he relied on showed up. Aaron, who was his brother, and Hur, who was a leader and friend. They found a seat for Moses and then got on each side of him to hold his arms up for him. As a result, the Israelite troops won the battle.

People will join you, as you stand firm. When I think about this story, I think about times in my life where I need to stand firm with my arms up, figuratively.

There are times when I get tired. When I get weary. When I get anxious. When I get fearful. When I wonder if I am enough. And in these times, my wife,

Angelmarie, comes. She finds a place for me to sit, and she holds my arms up. She encourages me and gives me strength. I get emotional just writing this and thinking about her support. Then, there are other friends and leaders in my life who come along on the other side of me; they hold my arms up, providing strength and encouragement. And I am doing the same for others. We all need people to surround us, and we need to surround others.

Sometimes, you have to stand-alone for a season. You will lose some old friends, but you will gain new ones. Don't compromise your ground or your convictions because of loneliness. Loneliness is never a good foundation to base a decision on. Rely on God's presence. God's presence is always better than people's presence. Psalm 118:8 says, "It is better to trust the Lord than to put confidence in people." Did you know this verse is centered in the very middle of the Bible? And God uses it to say, "Trust My process. Spend some time in the oven. Don't come out too early. Trust My way over people's way."

When you stand firm for God, He will stand firm with you. You may stand firm alone for a season, but He will send people alongside you for that reason.

Supernatural Advantage

The last part of this story can come across a little harsh. God basically said that because the Amalekites came against Him and His people that He would blot out the trace and memory of their existence! But like any good story, there is a back-story.

Amalek had made an alliance with other nations to come against Israel. Psalm 83:4 records, "Come, let us wipe out Israel as a nation. We will destroy the very memory of its existence."

A few chapters before this story we find the Israelites about to cross the Red Sea. Moses looked them dead in the eyes and said, "The Lord Himself will fight for you. You won't have to lift a finger in your defense!" (Exodus 14:14). The story goes on that they crossed the sea as God held the waves up on each side. After they crossed, God released the waves to wipe out the attacking Egyptian army.

The Lord will fight for you. When you feel attacked and surrounded, just know that the Lord is surrounding what is surrounding you. He will fight for you! The Lord is your banner. He is your victory! Let Him fight for you. Be strong in your life. Stand firm. Now is the time. We live in a culture that wilts under the pressure, but we are called to stand firm in the face of adversity and challenges.

Sometimes, you have to stand alone, but I believe you will encounter people who will make a commitment to stand firm with you. Make a decision each day to stand firm, and God will stand firm with you.

CHAPTER FIVE

FEAR VS. FAITH

"Everything you want is on the other side of fear."
- Jack Canfield

It was a warm, summer night in Texas. My wife and I had just finished dinner and I was taking the trash out to the garage. I walked barefoot across the concrete pavement and threw the garbage into the bin. As I turned to walk back inside, I remembered I needed to grab something from the console of my car. I squeezed into the middle row between our two cars, and as I prepared to open the door, I was stopped abruptly when I looked down and saw a spider just a few inches from my foot.

Now, this was not an ordinary spider. I live on the outskirts of town, just far enough that some consider it country. If you live in the country, you know that everything grows bigger in these parts. The wasps seem to have more nests, the snakes have their creeks, and the spiders are on an all-you-can-eat diet.

This spider was about two inches in diameter and looked overweight, honestly. I hopped over it and grabbed a sandal that was nearby the door. I figured I would see it again, so I might as well kill it now. I lifted the sandal, hit the spider, and it met its demise. I thought the scary part was over, but then a hundred little spiders came out beneath it. The spider was pregnant, and I had just induced its labor. (Go ahead and Google this if you want to verify my story.) I had not seen or heard of anything like this and I quickly headed inside.

I opened the door and shivered as I felt the cool AC on my skin. As I started to close the door, my loving wife scared the living daylights out of me. She had been hiding, waiting in the corner to scare me, and once I walked in, she yelled and jumped out at me. I responded by screaming like a four-year-old girl. It was not my manliest moment. Angel started laughing hysterically and has reminded me of that incident more than a few times.

Judge Roy Scream

Growing up as a teenager, one of the coolest things you could own for the summer was a season pass to Six Flags Over Texas. I had been to this amusement park a few times growing up, but I was scared of heights. Roller coasters were not my transportation of choice.

One summer afternoon, I went with a group of my friends. It was ninety degrees outside and the heat was just getting started. All my friends wanted to go on a roller coaster and they were persuading me to go with them. I hesitantly agreed, and we started on the beginner's level of roller coasters called Judge Roy Scream. It sounds much scarier than it is. But this was my first roller coaster experience—and I was petrified.

You know how emotions hit at an all-time high right before you do something for the very first time? That's exactly what was happening to me. We waited in line, inched closer to the gate, and when it was our turn, we got in, buckled up, and eagerly waited for the brakes to release so the ride could start. And just like that, it was off to the races as the speed picked up and we rode the ride of a lifetime.

I was stunned at how much fun I had. It was such a rush and I had overcome my fear of amusement park rides. My friends and I went from one ride to the next that day. We went on Mr. Freeze and then had our legs dangling on the Batman ride. The first time I ever considered going to a chiropractor was right after riding the Texas Giant. Then, we rode the climax of the park—the Titan.

The Titan is everything you would assume it would be by definition. It is over a mile in length with a mind-blowing 255-foot drop. This is all before you hit two 540-degree spirals back to back. We hit a speed of 85 miles per hour and 3 minutes later, we had completed the experience.

I had dreaded these rides for days. But by the end of that Saturday evening, I was in love with the roller coasters I had just ridden. I was hooked and ready for more. The experience was a lot less scary than what I had imagined it to be. Isn't that the way life is?

Fight or Flight

There are five types of fear: terror, panic, username or password is incorrect, "we need to talk," and twenty missed calls from your spouse. There is a good chance your pulse quickened at a couple of those.

Fear is the main obstacle of life. We fear failure, so we don't try something new. We fear rejection, so we don't apply for that new job, make that new friend, or ask someone on a date. We fear missing out, so we say yes to too many people and events.

Let's talk about how fear works. We are born with only two innate fears: the fear of falling and the fear of loud sounds. This explains my response after walking inside from the garage and being scared by my wife. When you hear a loud sound, you most likely will react with a fight or flight response.

Most fears are taught, but many fears are learned. Spiders, snakes, the dark – these are called natural fears. These are developed at a young age as we are influenced by our environment and culture. A young child is not automatically scared of spiders but will build cues to be from his or her parents. It's all about context. A child may not know that a skeleton is scary until his or her parents say over and over how skeleton decorations are spooky. The same can be said for scarecrows, clowns, and even those porcelain dolls that seem to be peering right into your soul.

When presented with something scary, your brain reacts with a fight or flight response. For example, if you see a snake while hiking, there are two roadways for your brain. First, there is the low road that represents your brains sensory systems. It is what you see, smell, and hear. Your adrenaline response causes your heart to beat faster and your body to sweat. Second, there is the high road. This is where your mind says, *I've seen this before and I don't have to worry*. It is the reasoning response that overrides the low road.

When your body fights fear, you begin to release dopamine. Dopamine is a neurotransmitter that helps control our brain's reward and pleasure centers. And the more you get rewarded, the more you want to do it.

Just Do It

A number of years ago, I heard a story about a man named Ken that I never forgot. Ken was terrified of heights. If he was in a building, he preferred the bottom floor. He would never go more than three floors up in high-rise. As he was driving, he would avoid any ramps or interchanges that would take him above highways at a high height.

But Ken was a man of faith and he had finally had enough. He was tired of allowing his fear of heights to consume him. He made the decision that he was going to get over it by doing what he was scared of.

He drove to the Reunion Tower in the heart of downtown Dallas. He turned into the parking lot, put his car in park, and started walking to the front entrance. He looked up and saw the observation tower standing 561 feet high. Ken stood and gazed upon the structure that is known as one of the city's most recognizable landmarks. Finally, he worked up the courage to make his move to the top floor.

Reunion Tower, affectionately called "The Ball" by locals, only has a top floor and in order to get there, you have to ride a glass-walled elevator to the top. It was the perfect place for Ken to go if he was going to overcome this fear. He stepped into the elevator and pressed the button for the top floor. His pulse quickened, and his palms grew sweaty. He went all the way up and then pushed the button for the bottom floor. He repeated this action multiple times. Ken rode the elevator up and down as many times as it took until he finally conquered his fear of heights.

Ken started living by a principle that day that I have adopted into my life as well: If it scares you, just do it. The best way to get over something is to take the leap of faith and do what you are scared of.

Are you scared of flying? Then fly.

Are you scared of germs? Then get your hands dirty.

Are you scared of heights? Then go to a high place.

Are you scared of spiders? Then crush a tiny spider.

Are you scared of the dark? Then go for a walk in the dark.

Let's take this to the next level.

Are you scared of public speaking? Then speak up.

Are you scared of failing? Then try anyway.

Are you scared of being rejected? Then put yourself out there.

Are you scared of commitment? Then be committed.

This all starts by you doing what you are scared of. Use wisdom as you go for it—but stop letting fear control your life and your decisions. One of my good friends, Ryan Leak, wrote a book called *Chasing Failure* based on this one question: *What would you do if you knew you could not fail?* You have one life to live, and it is what you make it. **Stop being paralyzed by fear and start walking by faith.**

What is Faith?

If you are going to overcome being fearful, it's not enough to just focus on not being scared. That won't work for very long. The best way to get rid of a wrong action is to replace it with a right action. You will not have time for the wrong things in your life if you are filling your time by doing the right things.

Fear works opposite of faith. Faith and fear are two different teams and they are always going up against each other. Faith is clearly defined and described by the author of Hebrews.

In chapter eleven, it says, "What is faith? It is the confident assurance that what we hope for is going to happen. It is the evidence of things we cannot yet see. God gave His approval to people in days of old *because of their faith*. By faith we understand that the entire universe was formed at God's command, that what we now see did not come from anything that can be seen...so, you see, it is impossible to please God without faith. Anyone who wants to come to Him must believe that there is a God and that He rewards those who sincerely seek Him."

This entire eleventh chapter of Hebrews is gold. Faith is simply believing God. It is putting your money where your mouth is and not letting your fear get in the way of your decisions. Faith is not the absence of fear, but it is the courage to step forward despite our doubts. The more you walk by faith, the less fear will choke the potential out of your life.

Mark Batterson likes to say, "When you live by faith it often feels like you are risking your reputation. You're not. You're risking God's reputation. It's not your faith that is on the line. It's His faithfulness."

It is your job to pray and believe.

It is God's job to answer and honor His Word.

When we do what we can do, God will do what only He can do.

How Do You Get Faith?

There are a number of different opinions on how you get faith. Some people pray to God asking for faith, some sing songs, and others just figure faith is not in their DNA.

A few years ago, I was at a church service on a Wednesday night. We had an alter time about three-quarters of the way through. The minister asked a number of pastors, leaders, and elders, including myself, to stand at the front of the room. Then, he encouraged the congregation to come if they needed prayer for anything. The altars filled, and a lady walked right up to me. I asked her what I could agree with her in prayer for.

She eagerly said, "Pastor Brandon, I just need more faith. I have a little, but I want more of it."

I asked her, "And how do you get more faith?"

She began using her hands, very descriptively, motioning as she told me, "You just put it out there and you take it back."

I chuckled to myself as I wondered what that meant. I listened intently to all she had to say and then replied with the following verse before praying for her.

Paul said in Romans 10:17, "Faith comes by hearing and hearing by the Word of God." That's the only way. If you want more faith, you have to read or listen to the Word of God. Faith is not something you pray or ask for. Romans gives you a simple prescription and it is up to us to do the rest. That word *hearing* is used in a continual way. It means hearing and hearing and hearing. The more you hear, the more faith you will have. And like anything else, you need to use and practice what you have. Jesus warns against the person who stores up what they have and does not use it for the good of others (Luke 12:13-21).

You do not need to pray or ask for faith. Just get in the Word of God and you will acquire faith. The reason you leave a church service or listen to a podcast with more faith than when you started is because you heard the Word of God preached. If you go a week before hearing the Word of God, you can expect that life will get hard because you're trying to get through the week with just a little faith. **Faith is what impresses God.** Stop praying for it and start acting on it! It's up to you to feed yourself with the Word of God. Remember, you are what you eat.

Praying in Faith

We commonly refer to Christians as "believers." I've heard many people say that believing in Christ simply means to believe with your heart. But if you believe something in your heart, your actions will back it up. Believers in New Testament times were called such because they said, and they *did.* There was no belief if action was not included. The core root of believing always entails action.

When I pray, I ask God in faith for what I need and usually include a verse of scripture to back me up. I also pray in Jesus' name because He gives me access to the Father. Jesus said we should pray to the Father and that He will answer us in John 16:23-24:

"At that time you won't need to ask me for anything. I tell you the truth, you will ask the Father directly, and he will grant your request because you use my name.

You haven't done this before. Ask, using my name, and you will receive, and you will have abundant joy."

One of the principles I use when praying is that I only ask once. Any time I think about it afterward, or if doubts enter my mind I will say, "Thank you God for answering my prayer. I know you hear me, and that you are working on behalf of your Word." A lot of people ask and ask God for the same thing over and over. But to me, that sounds a lot like nagging. God is smarter and wiser than we are. He has an excellent memory. He will answer in His timing.

If you have kids (or if you can remember being a kid yourself), you know that sometimes they'll ask you for money to go to lunch or a movie. You may say yes when it works for your family and you approve of the company they are with, and movie being seen. If you say yes, but don't actually give the money to them until they need it, would it be annoying if they kept coming up to you asking over and over for the money you already promised? Of course, it would be! You would start to say, "You can believe me. I love you and there's plenty more where that came from." I think it is the same way with God. He heard you the first time!

You may say, "Well Brandon, what about the parable Jesus told in Luke 18 about the persistent widow and the evil judge?" Is Jesus an evil judge? No. Jesus was saying that even this guy listened when this lady prayed. Surely, Jesus will! He closes by saying in Luke 18:8, "But when I, the Son of Man return, how many will I find who have faith?" Choose today to be someone He will find.

Who Believes I Can Do This?

Charles Blondin was a French tightrope walker and an acrobat in the mid to late 1800's. He became famous for his death-defying stunts.

One of the acts he was most famous for was walking a tightrope over Niagara Falls. Picture the scene in your mind. Niagara Falls is over 3,000 feet wide and 164 feet high. More than 75,000 gallons of water flow over the falls every second. The water hits the bottom with over 2,500 tons of force.

Hundreds of people would pay to gather around and watch Charles accomplish these incredible feats. And he would accomplish his task over and over, to the crowd's shock and awe. But from time to time, he would keep things fresh and change up his routine by walking across blindfolded or even on stilts.

One day, he showed up with a wheelbarrow. The crowd's curiosity was piqued and held their breath as Blondin slowly made his way across to the other side. He performed this stunt over and over and without fail, the crowd would cheer in absolute delight when he made it safely to the other side.

Then he would shout out to the crowd, "How many of you believe I can make it back to the other side?"

And everyone yelled in response, "We believe! We believe!"

Then, he would grin confidently and say, "Wonderful! Now, who will ride in the wheelbarrow back with me?"

And each time, the crowd would grow silent. No volunteers.

They said they believed, but their vocal belief was not followed by action. Religion says, "Believe in your heart." Jesus follows this by saying; "Trust Me with your life." Faith does not simply say. Faith moves.

David and Goliath

There is an ancient biblical story you've likely heard of if you've spent any time in a Sunday school classroom. This is the story of David and Goliath. It is famously known as one of the greatest underdog stories of all time. But when you really look at it, Goliath is actually the underdog. Things are not always what they seem.

David's brothers were in the Israelite army and his father sent David with some food to feed them on the battle line. At that time, the Israelites were in a stand-off with the Philistine army. The Israelites were paralyzed in fear at the prospect of fighting the Philistine's famed warrior, Goliath. He was a giant who was believed to be over nine feet tall. His armor alone weighed over a hundred pounds.

There was a generous reward for the man who could defeat Goliath and David was intrigued. He compared the risk to the reward, knowing the Israelite's winner would get to marry the king's daughter, be tax exempt for life, and become the hero of the nation! He responded to the offer by saying he would fight the giant.

Single combat was a very common form of fighting in ancient times in order to reduce bloodshed. The opening scene of the movie, *Troy*, is a great example of this kind of fight. But Goliath was expecting David to fight the same way he did.

David was a shepherd boy who armed himself with a slingshot. Before the fight, David had gone to the river and retrieved five smooth stones—and it was on from there. You see, David had defended his sheep by killing a lion and a bear in the past. But this time, he was fighting for God's country. David moved past the army's fear and walked forward with faith.

Imagine standing in front of major league baseball pitcher as he aims a baseball at your face. That is what facing a slinger was like. Except what was being thrown was not a ball, but a solid rock. Slingers could hit their target from as far as 200 yards away. That is the length of two football fields! This fight was like bringing a knife to a gunfight. Goliath never had a shot.

Notice one comment Goliath made while approaching David. Goliath said, "Come to me. Am I a dog that you should come to me with sticks?" (1 Samuel 17:43) It has been suggested by biblical scholars that Goliath had a serious medical condition called acromegaly, meaning he had a benign tumor of the pituitary gland. This tumor causes extraordinary growth in the person inflicted. Goliath also had vision problems, which is why an attendant led him to the battlefield. He never saw David coming![1]

David famously won by slinging a stone that landed in the middle of Goliath's forehead and planted in his skull. He fell to the ground and David came next to him, grabbed Goliath's sword, and beheaded the giant. When the Israelite army saw this, they pursued the Philistines and defeated them in battle.

When King Saul and Israel saw this giant, they saw someone they couldn't defeat. They were terrified. But when David saw Goliath, he saw an obstacle, not an end.

It's not about *what* you see but *how* you see it.

The Good Fight

In 1 Timothy 6:12, Paul writes to Timothy and instructs him and us to "fight the good fight of faith." Did you know that this is the only time in the entire Bible that you and I are called to fight? You are never called to fight complainers, gossips, angry people, or people with different political views, different religious beliefs, or anything else for that matter.

We're simply called to fight the good fight of faith. Do not stop believing. It is a good fight. It will get physical at times. You will get knocked down and bruised up. You will wonder if you can win. That is why it is a fight. You will get knocked around, but you have to pick yourself up and keep fighting.

Ponder this question for a minute: *What can God do through you?*

Don't allow fear to have a voice in your life. Fear is most definitely speaking to you. Do not follow the advice it gives. Choose to walk by faith, not by sight. God moves through people who move.

CHAPTER SIX

DESIRABLE DIFFICULTIES

"Boys step back, and men step forward."
- Fred Shuttlesworth

The toughest season of my life started near the end of year 18. It was August of 2006 and things were looking up as I had just started an internship in ministry and my first year of college had begun. I had graduated high school with honors that May from American Heritage Academy, which included being voted Mr. AHA by our faculty. I had enjoyed my summer break and was ready to hit my college years running, full steam ahead.

I was serving at a high school retreat in Tyler, Texas and we were playing Water Polo with the students during a break one afternoon. If you haven't played Water Polo, it's basically like Water Rugby where anything goes, as long as you get the ball to the other side. (At least that's the way we played!) I was having a lot of fun until I went knee to knee against an opposing player. As I grimaced in pain and crawled out of the pool in agony, I remember seeing that he was just fine. I was the only one who had been injured in the collision. I felt like I had broken my knee. I have broken about 6-8 bones (believe it or not, it's easy to lose count) over the course of my life. Breaking a bone can be like knowing when you're in love: When you know, you know.

One of the camp leaders brought me to a local hospital that night and they said the injury might require surgery. Since I was out of town, they insisted I see a doctor back in Dallas as soon as possible. Upon getting back, my parents took me to an orthopedic surgeon in Southlake. They took an x-ray and gave me the bad news. This was more complicated than just a broken bone. I had shattered my kneecap. Not only that, but there was much more going on inside of my knee that I had no idea of.

I don't remember all of the bad news that was given to me over the course of that year. I seem to have mentally blocked out traumatic portions of it. I remember too little, but my dad says he remembers too much. But I do remember the orthopedic surgeon recommended we see a man named Dr. Maale who was known as an end-point referral doctor. He is the last doctor you can go to in his field. There are only seven doctors like him in the U.S. He is at the top of his field in orthopedic oncology, sarcomas, and total joint reconstruction. Apparently, that's how bad my knee was.

So, off we went.

Bad News

Dr. Maale is a man I'll never forget and frankly, someone I wish could live forever so he could help everyone the way he has helped me. Dr. Maale and his team took x-rays of my knee and chest when I arrived to meet him. After the exam, we were led to a separate room with a couch and some monitors. I grew to hate that room. I found myself sitting there over four times the next year. To this day, my blood pressure immediately rises whenever I walk into a hospital. It's not my favorite spot.

The doctor explained that I had two types of tumors that were active in my knee and lower thigh area. He diagnosed me as having a chondroblastoma with secondary aneurysmal bone cysts. This was a rare bone disease and I was the recipient.

The tumors were all benign but still life-threatening as chondroblastoma has a tendency to travel to the lungs. Once on your lungs, surgeons have to remove the lung. We only have two lungs, so if it happens to both of them—you're dead. You get the picture. We were devastated.

My 19th birthday was soon after and I remember going to lunch with my family at the Cheesecake Factory to celebrate. I love that place, but I will never forget that lunch. It was the quietest, saddest lunch of our lives.

Not only was I an answer to my parents' decade of praying for a child—I was their *only* child. Watching them face the uncertainty of losing that miracle was one of the hardest things I've ever had to do.

That was, until I came face to face with the most difficult year of my life.

A Difficult Year

I had two surgeries over the next month. One in September and the other in October. My favorite memory from the first one was right before I was rolled into the operating room.

The anesthesiologist came in. He told me he was going to inject me with the anesthesia. I obliged, and he asked me to count to ten out loud. He mentioned that I would pass out before getting there.

I chuckled, rolled my eyes and said, "Whatever you say, Doc. I think I can make it longer."

I counted to two. And that was it.

The first surgery was cut short due to a cancer scare. They ended up just taking a biopsy because the tumors were acting abnormally. Thankfully, it wasn't cancerous. When I left the hospital after the first operation, I thought to myself, *Wow, surgery is easy. What's all the complaining about?* But the first one was only a 2-inch incision.

I learned the hard way in October when they cut a 9-inch incision over my knee that time. The surgery had two purposes. One, to remove as many tumors as possible out of my knee. Two, to completely remove my kneecap and the debris inside. To this day, I don't have a kneecap in my left leg, which has severely limited my mobility.

I came for my check-up multiple times in the coming weeks and months and all was in the clear. I was in physical therapy and working on my range of motion. (Can I just take a moment to thank all the physical therapists in the world, especially if you're reading this today? Thank you.) The two therapists I had were game-changers for me. I love them both, especially the one who helped me on this particular journey. Healing is a love-hate relationship as you are going through it, but it is all love after it's done.

April came around and I was making progress. I went back in for a check-up with Dr. Maale and he brought us to the infamous room again. My heartbeat quickened, and I began to get nervous. He greeted us in a somber mood and told us that the tumors were back. He recommended that I have a full knee replacement, so they could completely eradicate every tumor they could find. We didn't have much of a choice—this seemed to be our only option.

On April 23, 2007, I had my last surgery on my knee. This one was a 16-inch incision. They took my knee out and gave me a total knee replacement. If I remember correctly, they took part of my calf muscle out of my leg and attached it over my knee and thigh to add a barrier of protective tissue. So, my dream of having Greek god-like calves may not come to fruition on this side of heaven. But a man can dream, *right*?

Thankfully, the surgery was successful. The doctor woke me up and gave me the update. Very dryly, he told me that they had almost amputated my entire leg. I was shocked. He had not even mentioned the possibility. I was like, *Doc, I think that's something you've got to tell me beforehand—but maybe I'm wrong.* My leg had atrophied so much that they could barely fit the new replacement inside of my skin. I'm just thankful they did.

I was still recovering about a week later when my dad came home after a long day of work and a brief visit at the hospital. Two inches of water had filled the house and gushed out of the front door as he opened it. A small, very important piece of the guest toilet had apparently broken off and water had started to flood the entire house while my parents were gone. You know what they say. When it rains, it pours.

To make matters worse, over the next week, my sole source of entertainment was the Dallas Mavericks playing in the Playoffs. This was the year they rolled to 67 wins and my man, Dirk Nowitzki, won the MVP. If you're a Mav's fan, then you know what happened next and why I say it made matters worse. The 8th seeded Golden State Warriors swept the Mavericks under the rug in the first round of the Playoffs. I was ticked off with nowhere to run.

Rehab

I completed my twelve-day stint in the Dallas Presbyterian hospital after my surgery and then began rehab. I was happy to head home for recovery, but the next five months were long, painful, and boring.

The doctor wouldn't let me drive and we've already discussed how rules work in my family. So, my life consisted of physical therapy, online college, family time, and lots of TV. I will say, taking online college at my own pace was the way to go for me. I got my four-year degree in three years. Let's just say, I had the time.

Over those four years, my range of motion had gone from 130 degrees in my left leg to a whopping 10 degrees. Physical therapy over the next year brought my progress to about 70 degrees, on a good day. I had developed a little bit of a limp, to say the least.

Costa Rica

About a year later, in 2008, I went on a mission trip to Costa Rica with my youth group. The trip lasted two weeks, and I absolutely love Costa Rica. This was my second time to go and I am in love with the beaches there. The waves are big, and the scenery is gorgeous. They have one beach called Hermosa Beach, which means "beautiful" in Spanish. In America, we marvel over the white sand in Florida. This beach has the exact opposite. It is known for its jet-black, volcanic sand and it is a sight to see.

We traveled across a lot of the country on this trip doing mission's work in local churches and orphanages. I love mission trips for three reasons: One, they help us to get our eyes off of ourselves and focused on serving others. Two, they provide us with a great perspective of how blessed we are as Americans. We are blessed to be a blessing. Thirdly, trips like these can provide us with some great, new friendships.

On the 12th day of the two-week trip, we were staying in the capital of San Jose and I was speaking at a conference that day. The hotel we stayed at did not have carpet. Our rooms had marble floors, which sounds nice in theory, but as I rolled out of bed that morning to prepare my message, I slipped and fell. The toilet had overflowed the night before and covered the floor with an inch of water, turning the marble into slippery glass. My left leg went all the way back—which hadn't happened in almost two years. I thought I tore the thigh tissue right off my knee replacement.

I spent the day in excruciating pain and no one was able to find crutches over our last two days in Costa Rica. I had to wait until we were back in America. *How can a tour guide not find crutches? I was baffled, but like anything else, I thought, Let's just make it through with a great attitude.*

By the next day, no thanks to my tour guide and his lack of crutches, I was walking on my own again. My pain tolerance was on another level at this time. We arrived back in Dallas and I went straight to my doctor's office. He took x-rays again and royally chewed me out for walking in with no crutches.

He explained to me that I had broken my femur on both sides of the same leg. Surgery was not required, but the scar tissue that had built up over the past few days had basically eliminated whatever mobility I could have in that leg. And to this day, I walk with a limp.

Your Story Gives God Glory

Over the next few years, I had severe insecurities when it came to how I walked. I have pain at times, but I was much more concerned with how people perceived me. I'm not going to lie, it gets old when people ask and when people stare. It is what it is now. I've gotten used to it now. But at this time, my self-esteem was at an all-time low. I used to tell my story at length, but I have it edited to two sentences whenever someone asks me now.

Over time, I began to realize that everyone is insecure about something. Everyone is fighting a hard battle in some area of their lives. Many people have physical features that they are ashamed of—features that make them worry about what other people might think. Here's the thing though. People don't think about us as much as we think they do. They are busy thinking about themselves, for the most part. The sooner we can get over our own insecurities, the better.

Someone was sharing their story recently and this thought came to me: *Your story gives God glory*. God would not have put you here if you did not have a purpose. Your life is your story and your story has a purpose for God's glory. So many times, we shrink back from telling our story, but I want to encourage you to tell your story. Be bold and share your testimony with others. But remember, there is no testimony without a test. When you share your story, you are lending your faith to others. They will gather strength by hearing that you made it through. You can't be afraid to show your scars. That is who you are, and you have to stay true to that. You might have a limp, but at least you are still walking.

Sometimes, the only way out is through. You may not see it now, but if you keep putting one foot in front of the other, you will begin to see a light at the end of the tunnel.

Desirable Difficulties

There is a theory that changed my thinking forever when I heard it. It's called, "Desirable Difficulty."[1] Robert and Elizabeth Bjork are the two psychologists at the University of California in Los Angeles who formulated this concept. It will give a whole new understanding of how underdogs come to excel. The idea of desirable difficulty suggests that not all difficulties are negative. What could have been damaging, could actually leave you better off. The common denominator is how you choose to respond to it.

No one chooses to go through hard times, but we all go through them. There are things we would never wish for, but those things have the potential to help us become better versions of ourselves, that we may not have otherwise become. People who generally have it easy in life don't normally push themselves to greatness. However, the opposite of this has a peculiar effect. People who have had it rough—those who may have considered themselves unlucky or have been given a hard break—can sometimes push themselves all the way to becoming great.

The only way to overcome the odds is to have something to overcome. *Is anyone really an overcomer if they have no obstacles standing in their way?*

Obstacle Course

I ran track one year in high school. I didn't specialize in any one race, as you can probably tell by my one year of doing it. I tried a lot of different races such as the 200-meter, 400-meter, 1600-meter, and my all-time least favorite—the hurdles.

I competed in hurdles once in a track meet, and that was enough for me. The whistle went off and I stayed in the middle of the pack for literally fifteen seconds. Once I reached the third rung, I hit my foot against the top of the bar and came crashing down to reality. I started in the middle—and there I was in last place. Embarrassed and frustrated, I took off running at a frantic pace. I ended up finishing in 7th out of 8 places. I wonder, *is that considered a moral victory?*

The point is, you will have hurdles in life. You will have obstacles. And guess what? You are human, which means you will trip from time to time and fall flat on your face. You may not have seen the hurdle coming and you may be surprised by the turn of events to follow. But hurdles are like difficulties. You wouldn't wish for them, but maybe—just maybe, you should desire them. There are difficulties that are desirable.

Janna Levin, a Professor at Columbia University, was asked about difficulties and responded by saying, "I used to resent obstacles along the path, thinking, 'If only that hadn't happened, life would be so good.' Then I suddenly realized, life is the obstacles. There is no underlying path. Our role here is to get better at navigating those obstacles."

Choosing Courage

In World War II, the British government feared being bombed in London by the Nazi Germans. Their city is somewhat comparable to the city of New York City where the people to space ratio is extremely high. With so many buildings in a tight space and millions of people choosing to live there, it was an ideal spot for the Nazis to attack. Over eight million people lived in London at this time. The city was and is an important political, economic, and cultural hub. The British government feared what would happen should London be attacked. They thought the people would panic and their defeat would be inevitable if morale would collapse.

In the fall of 1940, their nightmare became a reality. Planes dropped tens of thousands of small bombs into the city over a period of eight months. 46,000 people died and another 40,000 were wounded. But the panic they feared most never came. Instead of panic, the people responded with courage.[2]

Where does courage come from? Courage is in some sense acquired. Courage is not something that you are born with that makes you brave when the hard times begin. Courage is what you develop when you've been through the hard times and you discover they aren't so hard after all. We are not merely liable to fear, we are also prone to being afraid of being afraid. In fact, studies show us that the actual experience we fear is a lot less scary than we imagined it to be.

Anais Nin said, "Life shrinks or expands in proportion to one's courage." Let's choose to expand rather than shrink. Everything we want can be found on the other side of fear. Confidence is not being absent of fear but choosing to be courageous in spite of our fearful feelings.

General William Westmoreland was stationed in Vietnam and one day, he was reviewing a platoon of paratroopers. As he walked down the row, he asked each of them a question: "How do you like jumping, son?"

"Love it sir!" was the first answer.

"The greatest experience of my life, sir!" exclaimed the next paratrooper.

But when he came to the third, the soldier's reply surprised him. "I hate it, sir." the young man responded.

"Then why do you do it?" asked Westmoreland.

"Because I want to be around the guys who love to jump."[3]

Learning Out of Necessity

History is filled with examples of people who had the odds stacked against them. These people had just about no reason to succeed, but we see them succeeding anyway.

There is a reading disorder, known as dyslexia, which is characterized by trouble with reading despite normal intelligence. Problems may include difficulties in spelling words, reading quickly, writing, sounding out words, pronouncing words when reading aloud, and understanding what one reads. These difficulties are often noticed in the years of learning to read in school.

These obstacles are involuntary and people with this disorder have a normal desire to learn. Dyslexia affects about 5% of the population, but up to 20% may experience some of these symptoms at one time or another.

A study was done on successful entrepreneurs to find what commonalities they had and what helped them become great in their field. One of the things they found was that an extraordinarily high number of successful entrepreneurs are dyslexics. One in three or more people have a learning disorder.[4] Learning came so hard to these people that they either pushed through with a high work ethic or found different ways of learning. They learned to think outside of the box that most people think inside of. They didn't want to learn this way, but they chose to overcome the difficulty they were faced with. As Malcolm Gladwell says, **"What is learned out of necessity is inevitably more powerful than the learning that comes easily."**[5]

In the 1960s, a physiologist named Marvin Eisenstaedt embarked on a research study. He went through the entire Encyclopedia Britannica and made a list of the people with more than one column written about them. The list came to a total of 699 people. The difficulties they had faced were staggering. 25% of the

699 people had lost a parent before the age of 10. 34% by 15 and 45% by the age of 20. And it keeps going further. 67% of British Prime Ministers in the last 200 years lost a parent by the age of 16. 12 of our 44 United States Presidents lost their fathers while they were young.[6]

Marvin's research proved this to be true: Difficulties can either make you or break you. Make a virtue of necessity.

Fred Shuttlesworth

There is a remarkable man by the name of Fred Shuttlesworth. We have all heard of Martin Luther King Jr., but we don't all know of Fred and his courageous life. Fred, a fellow minister, was one of Dr. King's allies.

On Christmas morning in 1956, Fred announced that he would ride a segregated bus. Later that night, the Ku Klux Klan (KKK) bombed his house. The Klan tried to do to him what the Nazis attempted to do to the British. As police and neighbors came toward his smoking house, a voice rose from the wreckage proclaiming, "I'm not coming out naked."

Moments later, Fred emerged in a raincoat and said, "The Lord has protected me. I am not injured." One of the police officers began to cry at Fred's humble response and begged him to leave town for his own safety.

Fred responded to the appeal without wavering, "Well, Officer, you're not me. Go back and tell your Klan brothers that if the Lord saved me from this, I'm here for the duration. The fight is just beginning."

The next morning, his church congregation tried to stop him from riding the bus—but he refused saying, "Heck yeah we're going to ride. Find you any crack you can to hide in if you're scared but I'm walking downtown and getting on the bus… Boys step back, and men step forward."

A few months later, Fred enrolled his daughter in an all-white high school. Angry white men gathered around his car, preparing to teach him another lesson. But Fred escaped, yet again. He was beaten up but got out with only a bruised kidney and some scratches. He told his congregation that he had nothing but forgiveness for his attackers.

Later on, he went to meet with Dr. King and again, the angry mobs formed. But again, he got out. This time, unharmed.

"Out of the way," was all he said. "Go on. Out of the way."[7] When you have nothing to do but overcome, you will overcome.

117

You Are an Overcomer

Each year, I have a doctor's appointment that I don't look forward to. I head back to Dr. Maale's office for an x-ray to make sure I don't have a tumor reoccurrence. His team will take x-rays of my knee and on some occasions, one of my chest to check out my lungs.

My best visit was five years after my last knee surgery in 2012. I was celebrating being 100% tumor-free for five years straight. It was one of the few times I have ever seen Dr. Maale smile. He looked at me and told me that once someone hits five years of being tumor free, there is close to a 100% chance those tumors will never come back again.

All I could do was smile back at him.

As we continued the check-up, he asked me what was new in my life and told him I had just proposed to my girlfriend, Angelmarie. She had said yes, and I showed him pictures of the engagement. He smiled again, bigger this time.

He said, "You've jumped over quite a few hurdles, haven't you? She's beautiful. I'm happy for you." And with that, he left the room.

You will have difficulties in your life. You may be left with a limp. I know I was. But the way I see it is that you have two options: You can either be overcome or you can be the overcomer. I'm guessing you're an overcomer. Let's overcome together.

PART III

THE TRAITS
THAT MAKE
THE DIFFERENCE

CHAPTER SEVEN

PREPARATION

"The secret of success in life is for a man to be ready for his time when it comes."
- Benjamin Disraeli

We've had a number of interns come and serve at our church throughout the years. I've met so many great young people through this program. I have a soft spot for interns since that was how I started out in ministry.

Last month, I had a couple of new interns start. One of the first tasks I had them do was to come up with a handful of things they wanted to learn in the year they had committed to serving. Once completed, they came into my office and sat down in the brown leather chairs across from my desk. With a youthful energy, they took turns and began to tell me the ways they desired to grow and what they wanted to learn over the next twelve months.

Some common answers and goals came across as they spoke.

"I want to grow as a leader."

"I want to be more confident."

"I want to learn how to do ministry."

But the best question that day came from one of the guys when he asked, "Pastor B, I want to learn how to prepare like you do. You are always so organized and prepared whenever you do anything. Will you teach me how to be like that?"

I love when someone asks a meaningful question. The question he asked was not a deep theological question, but it was a significant one that had the power to change his life.

Getting in Position

A young writer named Neil often speaks of one of the best investments he has ever made. You might assume it was some kind of monetary venture, but the investment Neil professes as his best was actually when he took a job as an unpaid intern at an American News and Culture paper in New York City called The Village Voice.

During the first year, many of his tasks involved opening mail and doing other people's expense reports—but nonetheless, he was so excited to be there. He interned with the paper for years and they couldn't seem to get rid of him.

Neil loved to write, but he wasn't very good at it. Because of his job, he was around some of the best writers and editors in the city. He admired them and spent a lot of his free time reading back issues in the archives. By doing this, Neil learned how to be a writer, a critic, and a reporter. When asked for his biggest failure, he used to say it was not getting into journalism school. That was, until he worked all those years for the paper. "This was my journalism school," Neil still proclaims to this day.

Neil Strauss is now an eight-time New York Times Best Selling Author. The years he spent in preparation put him in position to succeed.[1]

Have you ever considered what happens when you do not prepare? Things you hope won't happen do happen, and they transpire with greater regularity than the things you wish would happen. The reason is simple: being unprepared places you out of position. Preparation helps you to get into position for the future endeavors you will be involved in. Preparation helps you to become the person you desire to be. Ask negotiators what occurs at the bargaining table when they are out of position. Ask athletes what happens when they are out of position during a game. They will all tell you, they would inevitably lose. The separation between winning and losing is found when people position themselves correctly.

The groundwork is key. You cannot get to the middle of your story if you don't take care of the beginning. All great things take preparation. An ancient Chinese proverb says, "The best time to plant a tree was twenty years ago. The second-best time is now."

Don't worry about the past. Maximize the present moment you are in to prepare for the future ahead.

The Devil is in the Details

One of my favorite athletes is Tom Brady. I used to dislike him, but I read an article about ten years ago that changed my perspective on him completely. The writer described Brady's preparation and the work he put into his athletic practice every day. I couldn't help but admire him.

I was watching one of my favorite shows, The Herd with Colin Cowherd, this week. Colin was interviewing one of Brady's former teammates, Ty Law. Colin asked Ty, "What do you think separates Brady and makes him special?"

Ty responded quickly, "His attention to detail and his preparation."

Ty continued, "I had a front-row seat when he started, and people don't understand how much work he puts in on a daily basis. Whether it's conditioning, studying, or getting his receivers to go out to do extra work. It's nothing like I've ever seen. It is no mistake that he is the greatest football player of all time. He works at it. Age is just a number to him. He doesn't get caught up in the people talking about him being over the hill and being forty-one years old. Age is just a number and he is out there having fun. That is the most important thing."[2]

There is no such thing as someone being an overnight success. Their popularity may skyrocket in a short time, but it takes a long time of preparation to be able to succeed at anything.

One of the things that help people in their preparation is their attention to the little things. The devil is in the details. I have made many mistakes, but one of my goals is to not make the same mistake twice.

I will check and double-check my work and planning to make sure things go smoothly once they go live.

Next time you send an email, reread it to make sure you are communicating what you want to say. If you are responsible for a presentation, go over the little things involved. Is the PowerPoint set up correctly? Are there grammatical errors that need to be fixed? Is what you are wearing helping you to come across the way you want to be perceived?

It is the little things in the room that make a big difference. Or like my dad likes to say, "Preparation brings celebration."

The Little Things Become the Big Things

One of the greatest tragedies of the twentieth century was the sinking of the Titanic in the frigid North Atlantic Ocean on April 15, 1912. 1,522 people lost their lives during the first voyage of this ship. It is commonly understood that the ship's hull was ripped open by a largely submerged iceberg. But what if I told you that an ordinary key could have helped prevent this catastrophe?

David Blair was scheduled to make the trip aboard the Titanic. He was the second commanding officer and was reassigned at the last minute before leaving England for America. David had a key in his pocket to the crew's nest locker, which contained the high-powered binoculars that were used by crewmembers assigned to watch from an elevated perch on the ship for any potential dangers. Because the key unintentionally remained in Mr. Blair's pocket, the binoculars were unavailable when needed the most. By the time they saw the iceberg, it was too late. This ultimately led to the sinking of the Titanic.

If it wasn't for the missing key, the tragedy could have been prevented.[3]

Most people look for the icebergs in their lives and overlook the key. Many people overestimate their own personal Titanic and underestimate the minute details that help to pull off such a feat.

In the case of the Titanic, they unintentionally made a crucial mistake. There are times when we are warned and fail to prepare adequately.

Nearly a century after the Titanic, a natural disaster hit New Orleans in the form of Hurricane Katrina. About forty years before, the Flood Control Act of 1965 mandated improvements in the levee system that held back Lake Pontchartrain. The project was scheduled to be completed by 1978. Forty years later, only sixty percent of the work had been done.

The Dutch are known as having prepared their water channels for the worst storm in ten thousand years. Had New Orleans followed this example, no tragedy would have happened. It was a failure to not execute the prepared plans that caused this great city to go under water.[4]

There are times when we need a miracle. But I believe many needed miracles could actually be avoided by simply making the right decisions day after day. This includes choices in our monetary decisions, our diets, our relationships, and our careers. If you properly budget and plan your spending, there is a great chance you won't need that financial miracle. If you eat and drink in a healthy manner, you can increase your odds of being healthy.

The miracle is in the process. It is the little things in our lives that lead to the big things.

Champions Aren't Made in the Ring

My favorite movie growing up was *Rocky*. A lot of people joke about how many films they made in the series. They have made eight movies (so far, including *Creed*), but I wish Sylvester Stallone had made twelve. I just can't get enough of them.

My favorite scenes in each of the movies are the three-minute segments where they crank the 80's music all the way up and showcase Rocky training for his big fight. He goes from lifting heavy weights to punching huge slabs of meat and concludes by running up the famed steps of the Museum of Art in Philadelphia. When he reaches the stop, he triumphantly throws his arms up in the air and the scene cuts to the moments before the fight.

These scenes always remind me of what the Heavyweight Champ Joe Frazier once said: "Champions aren't made in the ring, they are merely recognized there. What you cheat on in the early light of morning will show up in the ring under the bright lights." If you want what normal people have, do what normal people do. If you want what few people have, do what few people do. The secret of success in life is found in your daily routine.

I heard an interview with Paul Levesque (also known as Triple H) this week. Paul is friends with Floyd Mayweather and walked him to the ring for one of his fights. Paul showed up early to watch some of the undercard fights that day and a member of Floyd's team came by to invite Paul to Floyd's room in the arena to say hi before the match. When he walked in the locker room, he saw Floyd relaxing in the couch watching a basketball game.

Floyd greeted Paul and offered him a seat on the couch. They talked for a while and once a lull hit the conversation, Paul politely began to excuse himself so Floyd could mentally prepare for the fight. But Floyd was enjoying the conversation and insisted that he stay. This exchange happened a few more times and finally, Paul spoke up. "You're not wound up about this at all?"

Floyd responded, "Why would I be wound up? I'm either ready or I'm not. Worrying about it right now ain't gonna change a thing. *Right?* Whatever's gonna happen is gonna happen. I've either done everything I can to be ready for this, or I haven't."

Whitney Cummings said something similar about her televised stand-up specials. "My work isn't done tonight. My work was done three months ago, and I just have to show up."[5]

You are either ready or you are not. If the bright lights turn on and you have not prepared, it's too late.

When Your Opportunity Comes

I worked at a coffee shop in Nordstrom for a couple of years after college. During that time, I learned a lot about customer service and serving people. It was a great place to work, but I have always wanted to work for a church. After my season at Nordstrom ended, I took what barista knowledge I had gained and was hired to start and manage a small coffee shop at my church.

I was twenty-four years old at this time and had been serving and interning with the youth ministry at my church for about five years prior. I was well known with our teenagers, but little-known in the church as a whole. Over the next year, I spent a lot of time preparing myself to be a pastor and investing in the people at our church.

I usually had Mondays off. On this particular Monday in March 2012, the pastors from each of our campuses had an all-day meeting. Our pastoral team wanted to have the Café open, so I came in to work it by myself. It was slow, to be expected since lunch was catered in. At the end of lunch, I had some business when people needed a pick-me-up as the afternoon meetings started.

Joel Scrivner came over to the coffee bar and said they needed me for a demonstration they were going to do. A man named Pastor Bill Scheer was training the group that day. He is a wonderful pastor of a great church in Tulsa, Oklahoma. As I walked over to the group quietly, he recognized me. My parents knew him from years past. My Uncle Joe Hanes actually led Bill to the Lord as a young man. He asked about my parents and my uncle. He then went on to explain the demonstration to me. Bill and two of his team members were going to interview me for an internship in front of all my pastors.

After the explanation, he walked back to his seat and the room began to quiet down. Some of the people in the room started to look my way and Bill motioned for me to come. I was nervous to have all of my pastors and elders watching me so intently. I sat down in a black chair facing Bill and his team and our pastoral team sat silently behind me. Things kicked off and what I thought was an interview felt like more like an interrogation as these compassionate men of ministry turned into FBI interrogators.

They asked me question after question with little time between. The questions and commands were personal and somewhat invasive.

"Why do you want to be in the internship?"

"Pray for ten seconds."

"Where do you rank yourself spiritually on a scale of 1-10?"

"What are you scared of?"

"What's your biggest weakness?"

"When was the last time you had sex?"

"When was the last time you looked at a girl inappropriately?"

The questions popped out like bullets from a machine gun. I had no time to think—just answer. And after what seemed like the final question, they abruptly stood up and we all moved to a different table in the middle of the room where they continued the interrogation.

"Fold your arms."

"Do it again."

"Do ten pushups."

I got down right next to my pastors' and elders' feet, as there was little room to move. One of which was one of my heroes who founded a great church and speaks to thousands each week. It was awkward, to say the least. I got up and they continued to question.

"Who is your best friend."

I replied, "Angelmarie."

They then asked, "Do you think it's okay that your girlfriend is your best friend?"

I sarcastically, but truthfully answered, "If I'm proposing in three weeks, then yes, I do."

135

They proceeded to ask, "How much did you pay for your car?"

"How much debt do you have?"

"What would your girlfriend think about this internship?"

They asked several more questions and then got up quickly again to head to the third and final area of testing.

They continued, "What did you read in the Bible this morning?"

"What did you get from it?"

"What is your favorite Bible verse?"

"What verses do you have for finances, healing, and salvation?"

"What is your relationship like with your family and with your dad?"

And with that, the three men smiled. "Wow. You're in. Great job Brandon!"

It was a shock to my system. Bill told the room that my uncle had been an integral part of him getting saved and the room went into an uproar. All the pastors and elders came to me smiling from ear to ear and shook my hand in congratulations. Some had tears in their eyes and several simply said I was a stud.

It was a unique feeling to hear the very people I admire say that they were proud of me. It was a special moment for me. It changed things for me. I was on the radar. I knew I had a calling and purpose for my life. I had been preparing in the dark for that calling and at just the right moment, God brought all of my hidden preparation into the light. Not only into the light, but God honored me in front of a room full of my heroes.

When I think of that interview, all I can say is that it was like being a sponge. In tough times, whatever is in you will be squeezed out.

I was offered a ministry role in my church three weeks later. What was most ironic about that is this: Bill Scheer was basically my ministry reference for the interview. About twenty-five years earlier, my mom was his reference for his first ministry job. That is God's hand at work.

Archilochus said, "We do not rise to the level of our expectations. We fall to the level of our training." Who are you preparing yourself to be?

Make Yourself a Man

James B. Garfield served two hundred days in office as the 20th President of the United States before being gunned down. He is the only American president who was also an ordained minister. Garfield is also the only president who did not run for the presidential office. The 1880 Republican National Convention was in a stalemate after the 35th ballot. James Garfield was not even on the ballot at the beginning of the convention, but somehow, he managed to win the nomination on the 36th ballot.

How did a man who did not seek to be president end up in the Oval Office? It traces back to a defining decision James Garfield made as a young man.

"I need to make myself a man," said Garfield. "And if I succeed in that, I shall succeed in everything else."

James Garfield made himself a man. Then America made him President."[6]

Tony Robbins once interviewed Nelson Mandela. Tony asked Mr. Mandela, "Sir, how did you survive all those years in prison?"

Nelson answered, "I didn't survive, I prepared."[7]

CHAPTER EIGHT

LEADERSHIP

"Leadership develops daily, not in a day."
- John Maxwell

Follow the leader. That is the rule I remember from kindergarten. All the five and six-year-olds would get antsy at the opportunity to leave the classroom. Our teacher would wisely tell us to get in a single form line and we would scramble and try to position ourselves to be the leader. "Follow the leader," the teacher would say. Even from an early age, we would jockey to be the leader or in first place. There is even a song about it. (If you know it, it's probably stuck in your head right now. I apologize!)

Leadership can be a broad topic. There are many books, blogs, and podcasts on being a leader and what leadership entails. We are not short on information, but we are lacking in understanding.

If you choose to recognize your own value, then you are choosing to display leadership in your life.

Desiring leadership is a good thing. This means you are willing to stretch your capacity and grow as an individual. Everything rises and falls on leadership. If you see a bad team, look at the leader. If you see a good team, look at the leader. The health of the organization or a team starts with leadership.

It Starts with You

Like anything else, leadership starts with you. It starts with your desire and continues with the action you choose to take.

I was seventeen years old when I first became passionate about leadership. The thought of becoming a leader began to pulse through me and I started doing two things that are foundational to leadership: the first is learning and the second is imitating.

I started reading books and listening to messages and podcasts on leadership. I identified people who had traits and characteristics that I valued and began to follow them from afar. You may not ever get the chance to meet some of the most influential people in the world, but in today's day and age—a lot of their lessons and materials are made available for us to learn from. Learning is the first step in getting ahead in your life. What can you learn from those who have gone before you?

Reading is a necessary step in continuing your advancement, both as a person and as a leader. I recently read that the average person reads one book per year. The average CEO reads 38 books per year. But the average CEO also makes 389% more money than the average person. This stat gives new meaning to Harry S. Truman's famous quote, "Not all readers are leaders, but all leaders are readers."

Then, I started noticing people in my life that I could learn leadership from. I had several leaders in my life that I could glean from. They were already there, but I was finally ready to learn. It's like the old saying goes, "When the student is ready, the teacher appears."

We all have people we look up to with behaviors we can mimic that will eventually push us to the next level we are trying to get to. All the greats in history have imitated people who have gone before them in one way or another.

Becoming a leader starts with a decision that you make. Leadership is not found in a title or position. There are plenty of people who have management positions but show few leadership qualities. But the opposite can also be true. There are people who don't have a position yet but show remarkable leadership traits.

You can become a leader wherever you are. It starts by serving those around you. When you serve, you are showing the heart needed to be a leader. Leadership is all about leading and serving the people in your life. When you serve people and make their life better, they will ultimately turn and do their best to make your life better. Most people will always reciprocate what has been given to them. It's known as the law of reciprocity.

Developing the Leader in You

Personal growth is the key to developing the leader in you, and reading is one of the best ways you can do this. The average writer puts about two years of their life in a book. So, when you read the average book, you are gaining two years of life experience.

It is much better and faster to learn from the experience of others than only learning from your own experience. Too many people choose to learn life lessons on their own, which only slows and impedes their progress. You can take control of your own life by choosing to glean ideas and traits from others. This will cause you to grow faster and with less difficulty than if you chose to only learn from yourself.

Winston Churchill read so voraciously while he was in India as a young officer that a biographer later wrote of him that "he became his own university."

Lincoln was also fueled by a hunger to learn. He read every book he could buy or borrow about the Illinois frontier, he enlisted tutors to learn from, and he followed lecturers from town to town. He was known to work late into the night to master a philosophy, understand a mathematical formula, or memorize a poem.

Benjamin Franklin taught himself five languages and formed a group of young Philadelphia journeymen who met often to teach one another in hopes of rising in society.

Thomas Jefferson taught himself seven languages, including Arabic.

Teddy Roosevelt's nightly ritual is a classic. The president would brush his teeth, jump into bed, put his revolver beside his pillow, and read a minimum of one book per night. He read 500 books a year—all while fulfilling his duties as president. He also wrote 35 books during his lifetime.[1]

In the 10th century, the Grand Vizier of Persia, Abdul Kassem Ismael, took his 117,000-volume library with him wherever he went. It was organized and carried by a caravan of 400 camels trained to walk in alphabetical order.[2]

These and hundreds of other prominent people distinguished themselves through ambitious programs of self-education and learning before ever making a name for themselves.[3]

Read Yourself Awake

According to neurologists, our brains have a storage capacity of approximately 2.5 petabytes. That would be the equivalent of leaving the TV running continuously for more than 300 years just to use up all that storage! Put simply, we have the capacity to learn something new every second of every day for thousands of lifetimes. And the three-pound supercomputer brain you have runs on less power than a 20-watt light bulb.[4]

You have a far greater capacity than you could have ever imagined—and it all starts with reading. A publisher once asked the 33rd President, Harry S. Truman, if he read himself to sleep. "No, young man," said Truman. "I like to read myself awake."

I find that the more I read in life the more results I accomplish. Reading keeps me motivated. When I look back at seasons of my life that were in a lull, I see that I wasn't progressively learning or stretching myself. I was stuck in a place of complacency.

Don't read yourself asleep, read yourself awake.

Elon Musk

Take Elon Musk for instance. When he had just come out with the Tesla and showed his friend Ray Dalio the car for the first time, Elon had as much to say about the key fob that opened the doors as he did about his overarching vision for how Tesla fits into the broader future of transportation and how important that is to our planet.

Later on, when Ray asked him how he came to start his company SpaceX, Elon replied, "For a long time, I've thought that it's inevitable that something bad is going to happen on a planetary scale—a plague, a meteor—that will require humanity to start over somewhere else, like Mars. One day I went to the NASA website to see what progress they were making on their Mars program, and I realized that they weren't even thinking about going there anytime soon."

"I had gotten $180 million when my partners

and I sold PayPal," he continued, "and it occurred to me that if I spent $90 million and used it to acquire some ICBMs from the former USSR and sent one to Mars, I could inspire the exploration of Mars."

When Ray asked him about his background in rocketry, he told him he didn't have one. "I just started reading books," he said.

That's how leaders think and act.[5]

Why Do You Want to be a Leader?

Take a moment to think about the following question: *Why do you want to be a leader?*

Intentions are the root of all decisions. If your primary desire is power and control, then you are not ready to be a leader yet. The desire for power and control are at the foundation of a faulty, selfish type of leadership. Leadership, in its purest sense, is selfless in nature.

Why leadership? The answer can be found in these two intentions: One, a desire to discover your own potential. Two, a conviction that you genuinely care about others. Leadership starts with believing in yourself and that God called you. It continues in serving and leading those around you.

Jesus taught His disciples on the parallels of leading and serving in Mark 10:42-45:

"So Jesus called them together and said, 'You know that in this world kings are tyrants, and officials lord it over the people beneath them. **But among you it should be quite different.** *Whoever wants to be a leader among you must be your servant, and whoever wants to be first must be the slave of all. For even I, the Son of Man, came here not to be served but to serve others, and to give my life as a ransom for many.'"*

We're here to serve. Leaders are people who take initiative in serving other people. We can easily be consumed by tasks. We must remind ourselves that it's all about people.

Connecting with People

Leadership is a journey. I have had my ups and downs with it like most people have. I've had times where I prioritized personal development and tasks accomplished over connecting with people. But connecting with others should always be our number one mission if we want to be in leadership.

Connecting with people goes hand in hand with developing yourself. I would rather spend time developing deep relationships, helping others, and speaking *to* someone than standing on a platform simply speaking *at* a group of people. Our relationships with the people in our lives are the most important priority we will ever have, second to our relationship with God.

John Maxwell says, "Leaders touch a heart before they ask for a hand." He calls this concept the Law of Connection.

It is easy to get so busy with our careers and what we need to get done that we start barking orders and overlooking the personal needs of those in the room. Be courteous and considerate as you lead people. Treat others as you would want to be treated. Use manners, slow down, and allow interruptions as needed. When you connect with the heart, people will gladly offer their hand.

President Bush

Four days after the collapse of the World Trade Center Towers, President George W. Bush visited Ground Zero. He spent time there with the rescue workers, police officers, and firefighters. He listened. He shook hands. He took in the devastation around him. He thanked the people working there and told them, "The nation sends its love and compassion to everybody who's here."

Reports said that the spirits of the tired searchers lifted when the President arrived and started shaking hands. Cameras captured Bush standing in the wreckage with his arm around firefighter Bob Beckwith.

President Bush spoke to the crowd and a few shouted out, "We can't hear you!"

Bush shouted back, "I can hear you. The rest of the world hears you. And the people who knocked these buildings down will hear all of us soon."

The people cheered. They felt validated. They felt understood. Their President and leader had connected with them in a way that no one had seen him do prior to that moment.

Four years later, Hurricane Katrina wreaked devastation on many Louisiana communities. People were restless to see how our government would respond as people lost their lives and others lost their homes.

As a response to the devastation, President George Bush flew to Louisiana. But instead of visiting New Orleans as he had New York City four years prior, the President only flew over New Orleans in Air Force One, peering through one of the jet's small windows.

To the people of the Gulf Coast, it was a picture of indifference. In the long run, the President did an amazing job of helping the people of those communities—but the image that stuck in the minds of those affected was the day he simply flew over. He broke the law of connection.[6]

Heart and Soul

When it comes to working with people, the heart needs to come before the head. What John Maxwell said about the Law of Connection is true. "Leaders touch a heart before they ask for a hand." Or as Teddy Roosevelt put it, "People don't care how much you know until they know how much you care."

Focus on your relationship and connection with the individuals you are working with. The more you do that, the more likely the follower will want to help the leader.

You might wonder about how to connect with big groups of people. Just start by connecting with one. When you connect with the one, you will connect with the audience and team as a whole.

There is a principle that I try to live by. It is a statement I first heard from Andy Stanley that says, **"Do for one what you wish you could do for everyone."**

We all want to help everyone, but the truth is—we can't. But we can all help one. Start there. Do for one what you wish you could do for all. Then people will know you are with them, heart and soul.

Who Are You Playing For?

There could be a number of reasons you want to be a leader. Some desire to be a leader to maximize their full capacity. Others have a genuine compassion to help people and make their lives better.

One of the ways I stretched as a leader was when I was newly married. Now, I am not only leading myself—but also my wife. In this process, I have seen that leadership is best shown through serving. When I serve her, I am leading my wife well. I don't just play for myself, but also for Angel.

Maybe you have kids and they are depending on your oversight and care to lead the way. There have been a number of adults who have started volunteering or serving in charitable causes so they can be a good example for their children. This is admirable.

Your reason for wanting to become a leader could be for a number of other reasons. But we all have a reason. We all play for somebody…

> *One of the greatest football coaches was Lou Little of Columbia University. General Eisenhower, who was President of the University after the war, embraced him as one of the greatest leaders he ever knew.*
>
> *In 1928, he had a reserve defensive end named Dennis Flaherty who practiced every afternoon with an older man. On the day of the game against their greatest rival, Holy Cross, Flaherty asked, "Mr. Little, may I start in today's game?"*
>
> *"Son, you're too small," replied Little. "I know you gave your heart out in scrimmage. That's why I sometimes put you in at the end of the game when it doesn't matter."*
>
> *"Well, Mr. Little, I've prayed. If I don't do everything an end should do, pull me out after the first five minutes."*
>
> *Well, the coach let Flaherty start and Flaherty played all sixty minutes that day. He blocked a kick, sacked the quarterback twice, intercepted one pass, and caught another for a touchdown.*

After the game, Little asked, "Flaherty, how did you know you could even play such a game?"
"Well, Mr. Little, that was my dad I came with every day."
"I gathered that," Little responded, still curious.
"Well, Dad was blind," explained Flaherty, "and last night he died of a heart attack. And so you see, Coach Little, today was the first time Dad would ever see me play."[7]

Leadership starts with you and continues with people. It starts with advancing yourself, but it endures with advancing others. And that takes time.

Just remember: It takes six months to build a Rolls Royce and thirteen hours to build a Toyota. Trust the process.

Lead yourself, and then you can begin leading others.

CHAPTER NINE

EXCELLENCE

"The way you do anything is the way you do everything."
- Tom Waits

I have worked closely with teenagers for over a decade. From speaking to crowds of young adults to coordinating events for them and investing time into my relationships with them, I can say with all certainty that they are quite an interesting bunch. A lot of people will ask me how I do it, but I think hanging out with teenagers is a very easy thing to do. (I just don't know how elementary school teachers do it. Those kids would run circles around me.)

Whenever I ask teens what their favorite class in school is, they seldom respond with the name of a class. A lot of kids, specifically boys, will answer, "P.E." as in Physical Education. Never surprised when I get this response. This can be the easiest class to pass, for sure.

P.E. was also my favorite class growing up because I am slightly competitive. (Slightly may be an understatement. I still race my wife on the way home to see if I can get to our house before her. That sounds childish as I write it out, but it's fun nonetheless.) P.E. allowed for healthy competition in sports while I was growing up, and I loved it.

Anyone who attended my school growing up would remember our P.E. teacher, Coach Giesey. This guy is a legend to us for many reasons. Not only was he our athletic director, but he had a gift of telling stories and drawing out the best in people. One of the things he did was develop an offseason program for those of us who wanted to go the extra mile. He called it BFS, which stands for, Bigger Faster Stronger. (Sounds like the Daft Punk song, "Harder Better Faster Stronger." It's okay, you can turn that song on right now if you want to.)

Bigger Faster Stronger

Coach Torres was another P.E. coach and another legend from my high school years. (It's interesting how easy it is to become a legend when you're impacting kids. You seem larger than life when investing in students.) He ran our P.E. classes, coached soccer, and was the overseer of BFS for Coach Giesey.

I was part of the BFS program during my junior year. Those workouts were intense. We basically did push-ups until our arms fell off and ran until we puked—if I'm remembering correctly. (That may be an overstatement too.)

A group of ten of us would meet after school and run with our coach over to the workout facility. It had an open-air vibe to it with a sliding garage door. It was filled with all the fitness equipment needed to build us into athletic specimens. We were legends in our own minds.

That program helped to develop all of us physically. We went from good to great shape by doing more than what was required of us. I was in the best shape of my life at this time. *Honestly, who isn't at 17?*

But why were we *really* in the best shape of our lives? The answer is because we went the extra mile.

The Unicorn Named Excellence

Excellence is something that most people hope for but few are willing to work for. We hope for the best but rarely work for the best. "Just good enough" seems to stand in the way. But like Jim Collins says, "Good is the enemy of great."

If you are going to fully recognize your value, you have to strive for excellence. Excellence is not perfection—it is the pursuit of it. Webster's defines excellent as "superior, very good, best of its kind, first class." Some of the synonyms are outstanding and exceptional.

Being excellent is one of the best traits you could ever have. One of the reasons excellence may be avoided is because of what it requires when no one else is looking. It takes time to be excellent and most people go home or start doing something else before they get there.

If you are excellent in the dark, your excellence will be brought into the light. Excellence starts in the small things and ends with the big things.

Dan the Man

I don't know of anyone more excellent in the Bible than Daniel. He is certainly someone to emulate. Daniel was 12 years old when he was taken as a Hebrew slave into the Babylonian Empire under King Nebuchadnezzar (Daniel Chapter 1). He was part of Israel's royal family and ended up as a servant in the Babylonian kingdom.

Within ten days, he and his three friends (Shadrach, Meshach, and Abednego) impressed the king more than any of the other men. He appointed them to his staff of advisors and found their advice to be ten times better than the wisest people in his kingdom.

Over time, Daniel proved himself more than the others and the king made him ruler over Babylon and chief over his advisors. Daniel served King Nebuchadnezzar for 43 years in Babylon and 68 years total. His life mirrors that of Joseph from the ancient Egyptian kingdom in a lot of ways.

Excellence has the tendency to inspire others to do more, but it also tends to make people jealous who are not willing to work for it. Excellence is available to anyone—but most won't go the extra mile required.

There are a few traits mentioned of Daniel that made him stick out from the crowd. What worked for him will also work for you. Daniel 6:3-4 says this:

"Daniel soon proved himself more capable than all the other administrators and princes. Because of his great ability the king made plans to place him over the entire empire. Then the other administrators and princes began searching for some fault in the way Daniel was handling his affairs, but they couldn't find anything to

criticize. **He was faithful and honest and always responsible."**

In the NKJV translation, it says, "Daniel distinguished himself... because an excellent spirit was in him." Excellence was the overall trait, but there were three attributes listed as well. He was faithful, honest and always responsible.

Faithfulness

The first attribute Daniel showed was faithfulness. We are around the 45-50-year mark for Daniel serving in the kingdom by this point. That is a long time. Especially when he could have easily been bitter or resistant when taken as a slave. Instead, he made the most of it and brought light to the dark. His attitude remained that way for decades upon decades. Faithfulness is easy to admire and difficult to attain. It takes time.

I was eighteen years old the first day I started the internship program at my church. I drove to my pastor's house and rode with him to the office. When he pulled up, there were about three guys who walked him in. This wasn't a normal occurrence, but I do remember it happening that day. They all greeted him

160

with respect, closeness, and friendship. One held his briefcase, another got the door, and a third got his coffee. In all honesty, I started out excited for the day but felt a little jealous that they were on the inside. They were closer to him than I was.

Over the years, we got closer as I just kept walking through the doors with him. I am more confident in my relationship with him now because I've been serving him for years, just like the guys I saw that day were doing. He is my guy. I'd do just about anything for him if he needed it. He believed in me when most people didn't. Now, I get to do the same for others.

One of the main things I did, during my internship and after, was just to keep showing up. I had a good attitude. When I messed up, I learned from it and moved on. You would be amazed at how easy it is to stand out in excellence when you just keep showing up.

Jesus talked about the importance of faithfulness when He told the twelve disciples a story called the Parable of the Talents in Matthew 25:14-30 (NKJV):

"For the kingdom of heaven is like a man traveling to a far country, who called his own servants and delivered his goods to them. And to one he gave five talents, to another two, and to another one, to each according to his own ability; and immediately he went on a journey. Then he who had received the five talents went and traded with them, and made another five talents. And likewise he who had received two gained two more also. But he who had received one went and dug in the ground, and hid his lord's money. After a long time the lord of those servants came and settled accounts with them. So he who had received five talents came and brought five other talents, saying, 'Lord, you delivered to me five talents; look, I have gained five more talents besides them.' His lord said to him, 'Well done, good and faithful servant; you were faithful over a few things, I will make you ruler over many things. Enter into the joy of your lord.'"

When someone made good use of their talents while the manager was away, he would come back and reward them with more talents. Jesus compared Himself to the manager in this story and us as those being given talents. What will we do with what we have been given?

Jesus ends the story by saying, "Well done, my good and faithful servant. You have been faithful in handling this small amount, so now I will give you many more responsibilities. Let's celebrate together!"

He calls the servant good and faithful. *Who makes you good?* Not us. Jesus makes us right with God. Jesus makes you good. *Who makes you faithful?* You do. God won't do that for you. You have to choose faithfulness. **Jesus makes you good, but you make yourself faithful.**

It can be hard to be faithful. If it were easy, everyone would do it. But before you can be faithful, you have to move beyond offense and being overlooked. Believe the best about yourself and others. Believe that God has called you to be where you are. Don't leave "just because." It takes faith to be faithful.

[handwritten: ✓ You can't be faithful without first havin faith in God's promise. You have to trust him in the process]

Honest

Honesty is another word for integrity. Daniel had integrity, and so must we.

Bobby Jones is one of the greatest golfers in history. He was the first player to win four majors in one year. Believe it or not, Jones was an even better person. He won thirteen majors before retiring at the age of twenty-eight, but it's the one he lost that set him apart.

At the 1925 US Open, Jones took a one-shot penalty, even though no one else saw him move his ball with the club. Jones was not completely certain he had touched the ball, and rule officials encouraged him not to take the penalty, but Jones assessed the penalty just in case. Jones lost the tournament by one stroke, but he kept his integrity intact. Winning the US Open wasn't worth a one-stroke penalty on his integrity. *That* is integrity.[1]

The army of ancient Rome used the word integrity almost daily in its inspection ritual. The commander would come to the line of legionaries, examining each man to confirm that he was fit for duty. As the commander came before each man, the soldier would pound his fist hard into the middle of his chest, just over his heart, and shout "Integras!"

The commander would first listen for the rich, full quality of a healthy soldier's voice. After that, he listened for the clang that well-kept armor would release when struck. The two sounds of the man's voice and the condition of his armor confirmed the integrity of the soldier.[2]

Mike Maples Jr. says, "Integrity is the only path where you will never get lost." Be honest in your work.

Tell the whole truth. Don't sidestep it. Be honest in your expenses. Give your best. Be honest.

King Solomon may have said it best in his book, *Proverbs*. "Good character is the best insurance." (Proverbs 11:6 MSG)

Always Responsible

Responsibility is definitely not a common Instagram worthy quality. It is not often people will post about their responsibilities. They may post about accomplishments, vacations, or events. I might scroll and see a picture of their dog, their summer, or their makeup tutorial. But we usually don't post about the mundane of our everyday life. Responsibility is not an Instagram quality, but it is a life quality.

Too many people overlook responsibility for talent. We might compare ourselves to people with more talent, but we can outwork them by being responsible. Tim Notke said, and Kevin Durant later quoted, "Hard work beats talent when talent doesn't work hard."

You want to be excellent? Be known for being faithful, honest, and always responsible.

Excellence in Everyday Life

You need to go the extra mile in life to be excellent. It's not always what you do, but how you do it. Remember, Tom Waits said, "The way you do anything is the way you do everything."

We need to define what excellence looks like. We need to define it for ourselves and for the teams we lead. If you don't define what excellence looks like for your staff and volunteers, they will define it for themselves.

Feel free to define what excellence looks like in your own life. I've done this over and over again for myself by using the following seven goals I heard in a message Brian Houston preached years ago—and they have helped me grow exponentially in faithfulness and success.

1. Do more than you are paid to do.

Ephesians 6:7 says, "Work with enthusiasm, as though you were working for the Lord rather than for people." You may have a great boss. You may have a bad boss. In both cases, work for the Lord. In fact, Paul said in all cases we should work like we are working for the Lord and not for people.

The church I attend and work at mostly is volunteer-run. We have many people who attend our services on a weekly basis and our servant leaders are the ones who make it happen. People are working 1-2 jobs a week and then showing up to church to volunteer their time. They are greeting people as they walk in. They are taking care of kids in the nursery while everyone else worships. They are running media in the back of the sanctuary. They are serving in the parking lot, so we don't have road rage before and after church. They are coaching and mentoring students. They are taking the trash out, resetting chairs, and keeping things clean. The list goes on. The point is, they are doing far more than they are paid to do.

One of the roles I have had for years is to become a youth pastor. Besides leading in that realm, one of the questions I often ask myself is, *How can I make this church better?* There have been ways and areas over time that I have added value to just by seeing a need and then filling it. Be the change you want to see. Don't wait for someone else to do it. A lot of the times, the thing that may frustrate us is the very thing that we need to step in and solve. If you see the need, meet the need. People who have learned to do that are hard to come by. Go make yourself invaluable.

Do more than you are paid to do.

2. Give a little more than you have to.

We are called to be generous. God's people are generous people. Nothing shows my heart like what I spend my money on. One of the things I spend my money on is enjoying a great meal with friends. Some may put a priority on makeup or clothes. All of that is fine. We put a price on what our priorities are.

Matthew 6:21 says, "Where a man's treasure is, there his heart is also." If you want to know what you prioritize, look no further than your bank account. We all have bills and needs but make a point to make giving a goal in your life. We can't give if we don't save. Have a budget or money set aside so you can give as needed. Tell your money where to go in your life. Don't make yourself broke but do stretch yourself. You are here to enrich the world and help others.

Give a little more than you have to.

3. Try a little more than you want to.

Some of the best things that you or I have ever done were due to giving extra effort—like working when you don't have to. When it comes to working harder than required, one of the best examples is found in the life of Nehemiah. He was an Israelite immigrant who served as a cupbearer to the King in the Babylonian empire. This story takes place a century after Daniel had passed away. Nehemiah made a bold request to the king asking if he could help his countrymen rebuild his home city of Jerusalem, as the walls had been broken down. He found favor with the king and his request was granted. (Nehemiah 1)

It is recorded in Nehemiah 4:6, that Nehemiah and his men had a "mind to work." These hard-working men built a wall in just 52 days. They slept less than normal, they wore the same clothes most days, and they built the wall while armed with a sword because they also had severe opposition from enemies trying to siege the wall.

Nehemiah had a vision of what he wanted to accomplish, built a team to help him achieve his goal, and stayed positive when meeting resistance. He also created targets so he could measure his progress and avoided distraction.[3]

Some ideas and projects in your life just need extra time and attention. Go the extra mile required to achieve excellence.

Michael Jordan once said, "I've missed more than 9,000 shots in my career. I've lost 300 games. 26

times, I've been trusted to take the game winning shot and missed. I've failed over and over and over again in my life. And that is why I succeed." If you try in life, you will end up losing at times. But if you keep trying, you will inevitably succeed.

Try a little more than you want to.

4. Consume less than you desire to.

This one might be the hardest for Americans. Practice discipline and saying no. Being full is better than being stuffed.

I heard a story once of a pastor who attended a leadership conference. There was a Q&A session with some of the world's top leaders on stage. A person in the crowd was given a microphone by the host and asked Jack Hayford a question. "Pastor Hayford, what is the secret to your success in life and ministry?"

Jack had a 4-word answer. "Make decisions against yourself." He spent time from there talking about making decisions against his ego, against his selfishness, and against things that might be second best. One example he used was about chocolate. He loves chocolate. *Who doesn't love chocolate?* But one day, about 30 years ago, he stopped eating chocolate. It started as a short-term decision, but he stuck with it to display willpower in his life. Just because you want to consume something does not mean you should consume it.[4]

Consume less than you desire to.

5. Help more than you need to.

Don't be a minimalist when it comes to helping others. Help more. Be a good Samaritan in your life. When you see someone in need, go be there for them.

There is a concept called the 15-Minute Revolution that is taught by Paul Scanlon. It is the practice of giving 15 minutes a day to help someone else. 15 minutes a day to be interrupted, distracted, diverted, or delayed. 15 minutes to add value to someone else's day.

We all have calendars and events to get to, but surely, we all have 15 minutes a day to help someone else when the opportunity arises.

Help more than you need to.

6. Waste less time than you'd like to.

Be efficient in your time. Spend less time watching Netflix and more time reading. Spend less time on your phone and more time with the people around you. Spend less time sitting on the couch and more time outside in the fresh air. Spend less time talking and more time doing.

At the end of the day, we are spending time—and what we do with our time is what we are doing with our lives.

Waste less time than you'd like to.

7. Give God more time than you're used to.

Start spending time with God daily. Slow down and open yourself up spiritually and internally.

Read the Bible. If you're new to spending time with God or don't know where to start, then just start by reading the gospels: Matthew, Mark, Luke, and John. Read a Proverb a day for wisdom. Once you read the Word, let it read you. Ask yourself how you can apply what you learned.

Spend time in prayer and in worship. Journal your prayers. Write down what you pray and what you hear from God in return. Prayer is not a one-way monologue, but a two-way dialogue.

God is not only all you need but more than you can imagine.

I am far from perfect. I have made more mistakes than I can count, and I am still trying to get better. All I can say is that I give God time every day. I read the Word daily.

God wants us to keep Him included in our everyday lives. Whatever light my life has is in the fact that He is the light within me.

Give God more time than you're used to.

Don't Wait for Someone Else

One of the engineers credited with starting development on a tablet PC at Microsoft was married to a friend of Steve and Laurene Jobs. When his 50th birthday rolled around, he wanted to have a dinner party that included some very famous guests. He invited Bill and Melinda Gates along with Steve and Laurene Jobs. Jobs went, reluctantly.

"Steve was actually quite friendly to me at dinner," Gates recalled, "but he wasn't particularly friendly to the birthday guy."

Bill Gates was understandably annoyed that the guy kept telling information about the tablet PC he had started developing for Microsoft. "He's our employee and he's revealing our intellectual property," Gates recounted.

Jobs was also irritated, and it had just the outcome that Gates dreaded. As Jobs recalled, "This guy badgered me about how Microsoft was going to completely change the world with this tablet PC software and eliminate all notebook computers, and Apple ought to license his Microsoft software. But he was doing the device all wrong. It had a stylus. As soon as you have a stylus, you're dead. This dinner was like the tenth time he talked to me about it, and I was so sick of it that I came home and said, 'Forget this, let's show him what a tablet can really be.'"

The iPad launched in January 2010. The usual anticipation that Jobs was able to rouse for a product launch paled in comparison to the frenzy that developed for this launch. The Economist magazine put him on its cover robed, haloed, and holding what was dubbed "the Jesus Tablet." The Wall Street Journal wrote a similarly lofty note saying, "The last time there was this much excitement about a tablet, it had some commandments written on it."[5]

Sometimes you have to bring it upon yourself to bring excellence to the room. Don't wait for others to do what you know you can do. As Tom Peters says, "Be the best, it's the only market that's not crowded!"

CHAPTER TEN

RELATIONSHIPS

"True love comes quietly, without banners or flashing lights.
If you hear bells, get your ears checked."

- Erich Segal

I'm going to start this chapter by giving you some really good news. I know the ladies will be excited and the guys will probably be thrilled too. Here it is: A new store has opened up in New York City and it is called the Husband Store. If you want a husband, you can go there and shop for one.

Now, there are some guidelines for shopping at this store. There are six floors in the store. Once you visit a floor and leave that floor to go to the next floor, you can't go back down. So, there is none of this *looking at all the merchandise and then deciding what you want* business.

One day, a woman went to the Husband Store to find a husband. On the first floor, the sign read:

"These men have jobs." She thought, *Wow a man with a job. That would be really good!* She pondered her decision for a while, but then she wondered, *Well I have to see what is on the second floor. So, she went up to the* second floor where she read the sign: "These men have jobs and they love kids." She thought, *Wow this is getting sweeter by the minute.*

But then she had to see what was on the third floor. The third-floor sign read: "These men have jobs, love kids, and are extremely good looking."

She thought, *Well, maybe I should just find somebody on this floor because that sounds really good.*

But still, she felt compelled to keep looking. She went on to the fourth floor where the sign read: "These men have jobs, love kids, are drop-dead good looking, and they help with the housework."

She thought, *Wow! This man has a job, loves kids, is good looking, and helps with housework. Oh, mercy me! I can hardly stand it.*

And yet, she had to see what was on the fifth floor. The sign read: "These men have jobs, love kids, are drop-dead gorgeous, help with housework, and they have a strong romantic streak."

But she thought, *Well, it keeps getting better, so I just have to find out what is on the top floor.*

When she arrived at the top floor, the sixth-floor sign read: "You are visitor 3,261,496,012 to this floor. There are no men on this floor. This floor exists solely as proof that women are impossible to please."

Now, before all the women stop reading my book, know that the owner of the store thought he should put a Wife Store across the street to avoid gender bias.

So, once again there were six floors.

Same rules. You can only visit one floor, one time.

On floor number one, the sign read: "This floor has wives that love sex."

On floor number two, the sign read: "This floor has wives that love sex and they have money."

Floors three through six have never been visited.[1]

Wifey Material

It's fair to say that men and women are complex. Well, women are at least.

Our relationships are a massive part of our lives. Neighbors, acquaintances, family members, friends, partners, and spouses all comprise our relationships. It is my belief that there are three major questions we need to answer in life, and they all involve relationships with God, others, and ourselves.

First, "What God will I serve?"
Then, "What is my purpose?"
Third, "Who will I marry?"

Who will you marry? That is an important question. Though it's not as complicated as we think it might be. It is also easier said than done. The person you choose to spend your life with will have an enormous influence on the trajectory of your life. Relationships are like elevators. Some take you up, but some take you down. Be mindful to choose someone you can go up with.

You may be single and not even thinking about marriage yet. That's fine. Just know that the habits you hold and the friendships you keep are forming who you are. The people you date and the experiences you gather are compiling together, defining who you are becoming, before you meet your mate. Every season is valuable in your preparation.

Or, you may be married and already have marriage down pat. If you are like me, you know you still have a long way to go. (Or should I say, a long way to grow?) We can all keep getting better. It is my belief that some of the same principles we recommend to single people should be kept after we are married. Whether you're single, married, or have the "it's complicated" status up on your Facebook profile, the following 10 relationship principles can be applied to all ages and stages of life.

Some Relationship Advice

I have a lot to learn in life. I can say that much with all confidence. That being said, take the following words with a grain of salt like you would with anything else. But I will say, I have noticed a lot of people are lacking in the relational maturity department and could benefit from the following principals. They might make good grades, have an admirable career, and make great money, but a lot of people are strikingly bad at dating and marriage. It seems that we think through our career and where we are going to live but spend much less effort choosing who we are going to live with.

For the rest of this chapter, I am going to give the best relational advice I have learned from my short time on this planet. It has helped me to become the man I am today, the husband I hope to be for the rest of my life, and the leader I aspire to become.

1. Hide His Word in Your Heart

In Psalm 119:9-11, David writes, "How can a young person stay pure? By obeying Your word and following its rules. I have tried my best to find You–don't let me wander from Your commands. I have hidden Your word in my heart, that I might not sin against You."

You might point out that he mentions young people at the beginning. You might also remember that David had an affair that turned ugly later on in his life when he had the woman's husband murdered. David would have been wise to follow his own advice. But as you know, lust and envy are no respecters of persons. They affect the single and the married. If you are single and still deal with lust, nip it in the bud before the stakes get higher.

Earlier, in the chapter titled, *Use Your Own Voice*, I mentioned how I use the Word to handle temptation that comes my way. It is a way that I hide God's Word in my heart. We all deal with certain types of temptation. Just remember while doing so, to use the Word of God at your disposal. If Jesus had to use the Word in temptation, you will too. That is one of the reasons we have it available.

The last thing I want to touch base on is the part

where David says, "Don't let me wander." Do you ever go to the beach? I love the beach. Any time Angelmarie and I are planning vacations we try and find a great spot on the beach. While there, I will always walk to the beach, lay out my towel and belongings, and quickly head out to the water to swim. But I tend to drift as I am swimming and hanging out in the water. I'm not focused on where I'm headed. I'm just having fun and trying to stay afloat. More times than I can count, I will notice that I have wandered about a quarter mile down the beach while I'm in the ocean. The current of the waves always takes me somewhere I wasn't planning on going. If I don't purposefully go against the current and focus on staying in one place, I will drift.

It is the same way in life. It is so easy to wander and lose sight of who we are and what we stand for if we don't keep it before us. We have to remind ourselves of what God's Word says and keep ourselves focused on it daily.

2. A Thought Does Not Define You

Have you ever had a crazy thought pop into your head? A thought that you would be embarrassed to say you had? We all have. Thank God not everything we think is broadcasted for all to hear.

A lot of times we think of temptation as a sin. But temptation is not a sin. Jesus was tempted in every way we are, but He remained sinless. *How?* He just didn't act on the temptation. He exercised his "no" muscle. We need to live lives not just full of power, but full of willpower. It takes both to be successful.

Martin Luther once said, "You cannot keep birds from flying over your head but you can keep them from building a nest in your hair." If you saw somebody with a bird on their head, what would you be thinking? *This fool is crazy! Why would they just sit there and let a bird meticulously build a home on their head?* I would turn and walk in the other direction.

But isn't that what we do sometimes? We just let thoughts come and go as they please, building nests of negativity and confusion.

Did you know that you have control of what comes into your head? You will have some crazy thoughts, but the great part is that you can tell them to leave.

It's just a bird. Don't let that thing build a nest.

Your thoughts follow your words. Your mind automatically directs its attention to the words you say. Learn to use and speak the Word over your mind and life to cast down those negative thoughts.

3. Be Kind

One of the shows Angel and I watch together is Ellen. She is a breath of fresh air. You can't help but smile when you watch her. Ellen DeGeneres always ends her show the same way. Right before the credits roll, she looks right at the camera, smiles, and says, "Be kind to one another."

The Apostle Paul reminds us in 1 Corinthians 13:4 that "Love is patient **and kind**." Love shows itself through kindness. Kindness in its purest sense is unconditional. It doesn't need a response. What would our world look like if we were kind, regardless of the feedback we received?

There is a popular show on Netflix that has made quite the stir. It's called *13 Reasons Why*. It can be hard to watch but it is also addictive. The storyline follows a teenager, Hannah Baker, who committed suicide. The story retraces her steps and the people who were influential to her low self-esteem—so much so, that she ultimately loses her purpose in life. When I watch this, I can't help but be reminded to be kind. Everyone we know is fighting a hard battle.

Be aware of how you come across. It has been said that your words are 60% body language, 30% how you say it, and only 10% what you actually say. We need to be better with how we come across to the people around us. People see you before they hear you. Be careful with the message you are spreading.

Dale Carnegie says, "The expression one wears on one's face is far more important than the clothes one wears on one's back." John Templeton adds, "It's nice to be important, but it's more important to be nice." After all, the golden rule is to treat others how you would want to be treated.

4. Don't Play Games

I am going to be straight to the point on this one. Don't lead someone along when you have no intention of being with them. If you need a game to be secure, you have no reason to be in the game at all.

5. Give Respect

The #MeToo Movement started in 2017 as a movement against sexual harassment and assault. Chances are, you could be completely innocent, but also feel uncomfortable whenever the subject is brought up. Experiences that people thought would be kept a secret are coming out in public.

I have a few things to say on the matter myself.

Guys, treat women with respect. Look at their face.

Girls are a gift, not something to be used. Be appropriate in your touching. Treat all the girls in your life the way you would want men to treat your mom, sister, or future wife.

Girls, be aware of what you are selling. Be modest. If you are throwing suggestive pictures online or in DM's, it is no wonder guys are coming your way. Know that you have the value of a princess. You are God's creation and His daughter. Present yourself that way.

Jesus said something very relevant to this in Luke 8:17. "For everything that is hidden or secret will eventually be brought to light and made plain to all." It may be brought to light on earth or it may be brought to light after life. Live your life like everyone can see what you are doing.

Live a life of integrity. If all your actions were displayed on a big screen or popped up on phones for everyone to see, would you be proud of what we saw? Live your life like everyone can see, because it's likely that they already can.

I live my life with a "healthy pressure." I am on the leadership team at my local church. I speak and minister to people regularly. There are people who respect and emulate what I do and the things I say. Honestly, I believe people do the same thing with you.

We all have influence.

I remind the people I am training and investing in of this healthy pressure. It is basically described as knowing you have value and remembering that people are watching you. You may go to the grocery store, a restaurant, or maybe scrolling down your social media feed. Wherever you are, know that you can run into anybody at any time. Would you be proud of how you are acting, talking, who you are with, or what you are watching? It's a healthy pressure.

I'll end with this question: How many times have you recognized someone in public and not said anything to them? People are doing the same to you. Give respect and act accordingly. Appreciate the healthy pressure you are living with. It can help fuel your purpose.

6. Establish Godly Boundaries

I firmly believe that placing yourself in a healthy atmosphere and around healthy, wise people is one of the best things you can do for your growth. You won't put yourself in bad situations nearly as often if you are establishing Godly boundaries.

A boundary is defined as a line that marks the limit of an area. What lines have you drawn in your life that are a boundary for you?

Sometimes people wander because they don't have clearly defined standards in their lives. You have got to have clearly defined things you do and things you won't do.

Some good common-sense boundaries can include the following:

- Don't text the opposite sex too late. Somewhere between 8-10 p.m. would be a good cut off. If you text someone later than 11 p.m., is it really necessary? It is safe to say that nothing good happens after midnight (or earlier)? I may sound like a grandpa here, but it's wisdom to keep your boundaries high and strong. I know people who are married who never text the opposite sex. I would rather be a grandpa who lived up to his potential than a young stud who has no common sense.

- Be appropriate when you give hugs.

- Look once, not twice. Let's be honest. God made plenty of beautiful people in the world. You will notice and that is fine. Appreciate what God has made, but if you look more than once, you're walking into the lust territory. We have a saying in my house: "Looking leads to buying." We use that as my wife (sometimes me), scrolls on her phone to look at clothes, purses, or furniture. I'll look over and say, "Looking leads to buying," if we have already met our budget for the month. It is the same way with relationships. Looking will never satisfy. Lust always craves more.

- Be smart about direct messaging. Some of you need to start sliding away from your DM's and into God's Word. You may need to delete Snapchat. I would rather lose an app than lose the purity of my soul.

- Use caution about alone time. If I were you, I would not hang out alone with the opposite sex in the house or even in the car. Let's be honest. If you still live at home with your parents, you are using your car as a mobile home or couch with your girlfriend or boyfriend. If you are married, hang out in groups when it comes to the opposite sex. Angel and I live by this rule and it has safeguarded our marriage immensely.

Let me close this segment with three statements

to live by:

One, if you have to lie about it, it's not the right thing to do. Humans have been lying since Adam and Eve and it's been costing us ever since.

Two, Warren Buffett said something about honesty that I will never forget. "Honesty is a very expensive gift. Don't expect it from cheap people."

And three, the number one question you should ask before you do anything is this: "Is this the wise thing to do?" Instead of asking about right or wrong, start thinking about what the best use of wisdom is. The Apostle Paul said that it may be permissible for you to do some things, but it is not always beneficial for you (1 Corinthians 10:23). Use wisdom in your life.

7. Be Aware of Your Online Footprint

Maybe this should have been the first principal.

Not everyone needs to know everything you are doing every moment of the day. 10,000 tweets are way too many. If your Snapchat score is over 50,000, go read a book. There are no social media awards on earth or in heaven.

In 2006, I had just graduated high school and a lot of my friends were getting on this social media site that no one had heard of. It was for college students only, which excited us. It was called Facebook. Everyone was on MySpace before this, but Facebook sounded somewhat exclusive as you could only join if your college university was listed. I lied and put a college I didn't go to, just so I could join the club.

If you have been on Facebook since the beginning like I have, you have seen how much it has evolved over the years. It started with status posts about how you felt, what you were doing, or where you were. It then allowed pictures, notes, photo albums, videos, and events. Now in 2018, you can do just about anything on Facebook. You can sell items, share news stories, or search for someone you haven't seen in 20 years. (I don't recommend the last one.)

Honestly, I was a good kid growing up but I am embarrassed by what I said on Facebook, how I came across, and how often I posted. (Thank God for the memories section so you can delete all the stuff you used to post.) It is common for people to be embarrassed by things they did or the clothes they wore 5 years ago. But Facebook, Instagram, and Twitter have become job resume sites as much as social platforms.

You can assume that anything you post on a social site can be accessed and reproduced for others to see.

I would rather not post enough than post too much.

As far as meeting potential people to date online, I would just be careful. There are so many stories of catfishing, where a person creates a fictional online persona for the purpose of luring someone into a relationship. If a world-class physicist can be duped over the Internet, you probably can be too.

I was reading the other day and was intrigued at how some successful parents have raised their children. Specifically, moguls who have helped create and shape the online world we live in.

Melinda Gates' children don't have smartphones and only use a computer in the kitchen. Her husband Bill spends hours in his office reading books while everyone else is refreshing their homepage. The most sought-after private school in Silicon Valley, the Waldorf School of the Peninsula, bans electronic devices for the under-11's and teaches the children of eBay, Apple, Uber, and Google staff to make go-karts, knit, and cook.

Mark Zuckerberg wants his daughters to read Dr. Seuss and play outside rather than use Messenger Kids. Steve Jobs strictly limited his children's use of technology at home. It's astonishing to think about this truth: the more money you make out of the tech industry, the more you appear to shield your family from its effects.[2]

It makes you think, doesn't it? As a general rule, it is wise to limit your digital footprint online.

8. Your Body Is A Temple

In 1 Corinthians 6:18-20, Paul talks about the body being a temple. "Run away from sexual sin! No other sin so clearly affects the body as this one does. For sexual immorality is a sin against your own body. Or don't you know that your body is the temple of the Holy Spirit, who lives in you and was given to you by God? You do not belong to yourself, for God bought you with a high price. So, you must honor God with your body."

Two things. First of all, "run." What does *run* mean here? It doesn't mean take your time, think about it, or jog. It means to take off running. Generally, when you run, you are running away or running toward something. Paul is saying to run from sin and run for your purity.

Secondly, this is provoking language. A temple was a sacred place, a place where the gods were considered to live, and a place where heaven and earth collided. The author purposely uses this example to challenge them with the idea that a person isn't just a collection of urges and needs, but a being that God resides in. He wants to elevate their thinking, to alter their perception, and to open their eyes to a higher way of what it means to be a human. He is persuading them to realize that there is more to life than just a quick fix.[3]

Remember, in love and relationships especially, your body is a temple.

9. Get Your Healing from God

One hundred percent of the people reading this book have been hurt before. Maybe from a father, a mother, a boyfriend, a girlfriend, or someone else in your life. We have all been hurt, abandoned, neglected, and rejected before. **Don't let someone's rejection determine your value.**

If you go from person to person for validation, healing, or approval, you will be disappointed in the results. Jesus is the Healer. God is your heavenly Father. There are things He provides that no one else can.

10. Choose Great Friends

It's the quality of your relationships that will

193

determine the quality of your life. It is not quantity, but quality. We have never been more socially connected and more internally alone. Choose quality relationships in your life. Notice I said choose. We need to associate with people who have what we want in our lives. Relationships are give-and-take.

It takes two to tango.

You are giving to your friends, and so are they. Choose and decide who your friends are going to be.

I deliberately stayed single, for the most part, in my high school and college years. I was picky, and I am glad I was. I made a few mistakes, but that is what makes us human. It was my relationship with God and my friends that helped me to keep going steady. Guys and girls: Friends are a gift from God. Utilize them!

I would rather have three true friends than a hundred acquaintances. It's not quantity, but quality.

The wisest man to ever live was a man named King Solomon. Some say he was the richest also. He penned a book called *Proverbs*. In Proverbs 13:20, he says, "Whoever walks with the wise will become wise; he who walks with fools will become foolish."

You cannot soar with the eagles as long as you're pecking with the chickens.

In Conclusion

FDR's wife, Eleanor Roosevelt, once said, "To handle yourself, use your head. To handle others, use your heart." Oftentimes, we do things the opposite way. We want to lead ourselves with our heart. We tend to judge ourselves by our intentions and others by their actions.

It's easy for us to lead others with our head.

Use your heart with others.

Use your head with yourself and your relationships. It's time we use the same wisdom in our relationships that we use in our daily lives and our advice toward others.

Here's to the best part of your life being your relationships. That is how it was intended to be.

CHAPTER ELEVEN

INVESTING IN OTHERS

"I'm a success today because I had a friend who believed in me and I didn't have the heart to let him down."
- Abraham Lincoln

Every now and then, you come across a story that seems too crazy to be true. A few years ago, I came across this story of Larry Walters and I have never forgotten it…

> *Larry's boyhood dream was to fly. But fate conspired to keep him from his dream. He joined the Air Force, but his poor eyesight disqualified him from the job of a pilot. After he was discharged from the military, he sat in his backyard watching jets fly overhead.*
> *He hatched his weather balloon scheme while sitting outside in his "extremely comfortable" Sears lawn chair. He purchased 45*

weather balloons from an army-navy surplus store, tied them to his tethered lawn chair dubbed the Inspiration I, and filled the 4-foot diameter balloons with helium. Then he strapped himself into his lawn chair with some sandwiches, Miller Light, and a pellet gun. He figured he would pop a few of the many balloons when it was time to descend.

Larry's plan was to sever the anchor and lazily float up to a height of about 30 feet above his backyard where he would enjoy a few hours of flight before coming back down. But things didn't work out as Larry planned.

When his friends cut the cord anchoring the lawn chair to his Jeep, he did not float lazily up to 30 feet. Instead, he streaked into the LA skies as if shot from a cannon, pulled by a lift of 42 helium balloons holding 33 cubic feet of helium each. He didn't level off at 100 feet, nor did he level off at 1,000 feet. After climbing and climbing, he leveled off at 16,000 feet.

At that height, he felt he could not risk shooting any of the balloons, lest he unbalance the load and find himself in real trouble. So he stayed there, drifting cold and frightened with his beer

*and sandwiches, for more than 14 hours. He
crossed the primary approach corridor of LAX,
where Trans World Airlines and Delta Airlines
pilots radioed in reports of the strange sight.
Eventually, he gathered the nerve to shoot a
few balloons and slowly descended. The
hanging tethers tangled and caught in a power
line, blacking out a Long Beach neighborhood
for 20 minutes. Larry climbed to safety, where he
was arrested by waiting members of the LAPD.
As he was led away in handcuffs, a reporter
dispatched to cover the daring rescue asked him
why he had done it.*
*Larry replied nonchalantly, "A man can't just sit
around."*[1]

The Reason You Are Here

One of the last things Jesus said before He ascended
to heaven was, "Go and make disciples." Last I
checked, that hasn't changed. Your purpose in life can
be found in your relationships. One of the predominant
reasons we are here is to help, empower, and invest in
other people. If all I needed were to be close to God, I
would be in heaven by now. And it would be a whole
lot easier there than here.

The religious leaders in ancient Jewish times were a group that called themselves Pharisees. They had a list of 613 Commandments and laws that they had to keep. I think you will agree with me that those are way too many rules.

One day, they tried to trap Jesus in front of a group of people by asking Him what the most important commandment was. In a nutshell, He responded by saying that there are two commandments tied for first place. The first is to love God. The second is to love people. In fact, to love them as you love yourself. That is a lot of love!

The proof that I love God can be found in the way that I love people.

The Boomerang Principle

People are the most precious commodity under heaven. There is a principle I once heard John Maxwell speak of called the Boomerang Principle. A boomerang is a curved, wooden Australian tool that returns to the thrower once released. Similarly, Maxwell's Boomerang Principle states that when we help others, we help ourselves. When you invest in others, you will inevitably be invested in yourself.

One of the most famous women of the last

century is Helen Keller. One of the most overlooked women of the last century may be Anne Sullivan. Helen Keller contracted an illness when she was 19 months old causing her to become blind and deaf. She was someone most people would have overlooked. Anne Sullivan came into Helen Keller's life at the age of seven. She brought the world to life for Helen and taught her how to communicate with the people around her.

Helen Keller was the first blind and deaf person in America's history that not only went to college but completed it with her Bachelor of Arts degree. Many did not believe Helen would do great things with her life, but she did not allow her disabilities to define her. She exceeded expectations and became a world-renowned speaker and author.

Later in life, Anne Sullivan became very ill and needed a caretaker of her own. Who do you think took care of her? None other than Helen Keller. The investor became the one who needed help and the one to whom she had added value turned and gave value to her.

Like a boomerang, when you invest in others, it will come back to you—sometimes in the most unforeseen way.

Andrew Carnegie, one of the richest and most successful men in American business, said it like this: "No man becomes rich unless he enriches others."

Takers, Traders, and Investors

John Maxwell discusses a concept in his book, *Winning with People*, that I want to share with you. This concept will help you assess how you currently operate in your relationships. First, let's note that there are three kinds of people when it comes to investing in relationships: *takers*, *traders*, and *investors*.

1. **Takers** receive and never give. Many people focus on themselves and rarely go out of their way to do anything for other people. Takers worry only about what they can get, and they are never satisfied.

2. **Traders** receive and then give. Most people find themselves here because our society is based on a bartering or trading mentality. You give me something, I give you something. This is how life works. Some people focus on keeping score. Their primary motivation isn't to help others, but they see relationships as a

conditional exchange. They are mere reciprocators.

3. Investors give and then receive. They focus on others. They desire to make everything and everyone they touch better. They understand the best way to accomplish that is to give of themselves. Ironically, they win the most in relationships.

So, are you a taker, a trader, or an investor? President Woodrow Wilson once said, "You are here to enrich the world and you impoverish yourself if you forget the errand." One of the best investors we see in the Bible is Paul. When writing to the church of Philippi, he mentions one of his favorite people to invest in, Timothy. Philippians 2:19-22 says this:

"If the Lord Jesus is willing, I hope to send Timothy to you soon for a visit. Then he can cheer me up by telling me how you are getting along. I have no one else like Timothy, who genuinely cares about your welfare. All the others care only for themselves and not for what matters to Jesus Christ. But you know how Timothy has proved himself. Like a son with his father,

he has served with me in preaching the Good News."

All throughout the Bible, we see people investing in others.

Moses invested in Joshua and Caleb. Moses was leading up to two million people to the Promised Land and he took the time to invest in twelve people. Two of twelve stood out, and they are the ones whose names we remember. Joshua even ended up leading the people of Israel after Moses. (Numbers 13)

Naomi invested in Ruth. Naomi was a lady that not many people knew. Her husband passed away along with her two sons. She invested in her two daughters-in-law and one of them stayed to return the investment. We know her as Ruth, the great-grandmother of one of the most celebrated kings of all time, King David. (Ruth 1, Matthew 1:5-6)

Elijah invested in Elisha. Elisha asked for a double portion of what Elijah had and he received it. (2 Kings 2:9)

Paul invested into Timothy.

Jesus invested in His disciples.

But who are we investing in?

Take a Chance on Me

I have been blessed to have two spiritual fathers in my life. One is my dad, who has been my greatest friend in my life, outside of my wife, Angelmarie. It was an incredible honor to have him be my best man in my wedding. (There is hope parents. Keep on training your kids the right way. It will take eventually).

I grew up attending Christian schools where we had Bible classes five days a week and chapel one day a week. The youth pastor at that time was a man named Joel Scrivner. He was the pastor who spoke at most of our chapels and helped to mentor many of us.

He heard me speak at a chapel service toward the end of my senior year and took me to lunch to talk about it. I felt like the cool kid in school that day for two reasons. One, I got to eat off-campus with Pastor Joel. Two, I got to miss two periods of classes that day. It was our first time having lunch together and he introduced me to Asian food. Hello, *Pei Wei*! (I have since received my degree in Asian Culinary, or so it feels.)

One of the questions he asked me at lunch that day was one of the more common questions I was getting at that time. "What are you going to do for college?"

I knew then that I wanted to be a pastor in the future. I told him my plan was to stay in town for the next two years to get my associate's degree and then move to Tulsa, Oklahoma to attend Bible college and join an internship at a local church.

He answered by saying, "Well, if you're going to be here for two years, what do you think about interning with me? You can serve with me in the youth group and I can show you how to do ministry."

To say I was excited at the opportunity would be an understatement.

I started working with Pastor Joel in July of 2006 and I am still working with him in ministry as I write this in August of 2018. My original two-year plan changed as I realized it would have been useless for me to go anywhere else. I was being mentored and trained for ministry right where I was. I had found a church home, senior pastors I could serve under, and a leader who invested in me. Pastor Joel saw things in me that I did not see in myself. He trained and developed me. He took the time to invest in me.

Who Are You Investing In?

Something incredible happens in you when you are invested in. You become an investor yourself.

I became an investor after I was invested in. I feel indebted to do so because of what leaders saw in me when I was young. Investing in others is not something you have to do, but something you get to do. Somebody believed in me and I want to be the one who believes in others. I want to be the voice who sees and calls out the greatness in another person's life. Abraham Lincoln, when asked about how he became great leader he was, stated, "I'm a success today because I had a friend who believed in me and I didn't have the heart to let him down."

Who is in your life that you can disciple and invest in? Who is at your job that you can influence? Who is living in your house that you can mentor? Who is in your community that you can build a relationship with? Who is at your church that you can love? You have the goods. You might think that you don't have what it takes, but you do.

You have people in your life who are looking up to you as a leader in their lives. You are someone they can follow. They might just be scared to tell you. They don't know what to say or do. That's why I tell the students in our youth group and those I influence in any way, "Go and get a mentor. It is the best and fastest way for you to become the person God has created you to be."

    If you're looking for a mentor in your life, find someone you admire and look up to and ask if you can meet with them for one hour, one day a month. Buy them food or take them to get coffee. Come ready with questions to ask. Take notes and show them you are ready to learn.

    Then, once you have been developed, go and find someone that you can develop and mentor. Pay it forward.

Mentors Matter

We were in a staff meeting a few months back when our campus pastor told the staff about the first time we had lunch together. He told them I came to that lunch with a notebook, a pen, and questions to ask him. Then I wrote everything he said down. He mentioned that he immediately took note of me because hardly anyone would ever do that.

    When you show that you are serious about learning and improving yourself, people will take the time and energy to invest in you.

    One of the most important things you can do to improve your life is to find a good mentor. If you want

to win in life and gain an advantag
influence, get a mentor. Mentors c
are ahead of you in business or sor
characteristics and qualities you ad

Find a mentor for all areas of your life—your spirituality, your career, your health, your money, and your marriage. I have been married for six years now, and do you know who I'm not going to for advice on marriage? Someone who is single, or someone who has only been married as long as me. I want advice from people who have been married for twenty to forty years. Someone who actually knows what they are doing and has proved it by living it out.

If I need money advice, I am not going to ask someone who spends more than they earn. I am going to ask someone who is wise with their money. If I need spiritual advice, it is going to be from someone I look up to in that realm. If I want to be a leader, then I will hang around leaders.

In the same way, there are people who want what you have, and they can learn from you. You're not too young and you're not too old. If you are reading these words, you can make a difference. All we're waiting on is for you or them to act. The world needs better people and you can make a difference by becoming a better version of yourself.

Mentorship is not always about asking questions and receiving answers. Oftentimes, it is just about doing life with someone you admire and respect. I have done just about everything with my mentor. I have gone to the grocery store with him, to meetings, gone swimming—and we just do life together. When I told Joel that I liked Angelmarie before we started dating, it was in his pool. We were simply doing life together. He didn't mentor me by sitting me down in his office to explain the Bible to me 24/7. He showed me the Bible through his life. Who can we invest ourselves into?

Empty Cups

There are a lot of people I have invested in. I will mention a few. When I was relatively new in my role in youth ministry, I remember telling our campus pastor about the four best student leaders across all of our church campuses. I would often think about what I could do if I just had one of them working for me.

One day, one of the four students came to a service. My wife and I made her feel welcomed and included. We would have done that to anyone, but

210

especially her. Her name is Stephanee. I considered her boyfriend at the time (now fiancé, c'mon somebody) to be one of the four best as well. His name is Josh. Long story short, they both came to our campus and became leaders with us. This was four years ago, and they are still serving at our church today. They went from being student leaders to adult leaders and are now serving as staff members at our church.

Cassius is another friend we've mentored. Ten years ago, he started coming to our church to meet girls. That might sound like a bad idea, but it shows his wisdom. The best people on the planet can be found at church. He joined my high school seniors' small group as a junior. He was a knucklehead. Have you ever met someone who rubbed you the wrong way? That was Cassius.

One day, Pastor Joel was praying in service and spoke an encouraging word over Cassius. When he ended his prayer, he asked me to help get Cassius connected. I said yes out loud as I nodded in agreement, but inside my head, I was thinking, *That's not going to happen. He's not here for the right reasons. We don't really get along easily so I'm not going to invest in this one. I did a bad job as a leader in this case.*

About a year later, Cassius texted me and told me that because of my influence in his life, he had decided to become a Christian. I thought he had texted the wrong guy! Sometimes we can feel like we are failing as a leader, a parent, or a friend. However, God can use us in spite of ourselves.

An old Spanish Proverb says, **"More grows in the garden than the gardener knows he has sown."** You don't have to do a perfect job. Even when we feel like we are failing, we can be succeeding with those around us. Cassius and I have grown to be great friends. He is one of my favorite people in the world. He is one of the speakers and leaders in our youth ministry.

Not every person will turn out that way. They won't all respond the way you want them to, but their response is not your job. It will get frustrating sometimes, but your purpose, through Christ, can be found in the people you are serving with your life.

It's not my job to fill your cup, but it is my job to empty my cup.

God will take care of the person who invests in others! Find someone to serve. Find others to do life with. Find others to invest in.

It Is the People Who Count

In ancient times, Jewish rabbis were considered to be the spiritual leaders of Israel. One story speaks of a rabbi who was especially revered.

A student asked the rabbi a question toward the end of his life saying, "Rabbi, who has taught you the most in your life?"

The rabbi paused, looked at his student and answered, "I have learned a lot from my teachers and rabbis who trained me in the way I should go. I have learned even more from my peers who I do life with. But I have grown the most from my students. They have caused me to become greater than I thought I could be."

One of the best ways you can grow is by helping others grow. You will find that by helping others, you are helped too. Our purpose is found in serving God's people. When we love people, we are loving God.

Some years ago, Alice Freeman Palmer, the President of Wesley College, was told by her husband that she should retire and devote herself to writing. She rejected this advice by saying, "It is the people that count. You want to put yourself into people. They touch other people, these others still, and so you go on working forever."

Who has God placed in your life to develop and disciple? Go and ask them if you can disciple and mentor them. They will be encouraged to know the potential you see in them. May you say, like Paul did, "Follow me as I follow Christ!" (1 Corinthians 11:1)

Go be an investor today. Find the ones you need to develop. They might just recognize their own value once you recognize yours.

CHAPTER TWELVE

CONCLUSION

My goal for writing this book is that you would go and change your world. Before you do, let me leave you with my final thoughts on valuing yourself.

1. Create yourself.

We often hear that we need to discover ourselves. People may go to retreats, start hobbies, ask for other's opinions, and more—just to find their purpose. We are desperate to find ourselves. I would say, "Look no further than the mirror if you wish to find yourself."

There is some value in the discovering, but it is mostly focused on looking at the past. If you were driving a car that would be the equivalent of looking out the rearview mirror. Looking out the front windshield is how you get where you want to go in life.

Instead of spending so much time discovering, spend your time creating. What do you want your life to look like? For the most part, you absolutely get to choose!

Dream, set goals, and go make your dream-life happen. You only live once.

2. Don't sell yourself short.

If you are worth God's time in creating you, you are worth the time of others. Many times we think, *Oh they don't have time for me.* Let me correct that mindset. You are absolutely worthy and worth people's time of day. Set the bar high. Put to use the gifting and personality that you have inside of you. The world needs you.

3. Don't overestimate the people on pedestals.

The people who have made a great impact on society in the past are not that different from you. They were a lot like you when they got started, so there is nothing stopping the rest of us from doing the same thing. Steve Jobs gave some profound words in a 1995 interview. He said, "Life can be so much broader once you discover one simple fact, and that is that **everything around you that you call 'life' was made up by people that were no smarter than you.** And you can change it, you can influence it, you can build your own things that other people can use. Once you learn that, you'll never be the same again."

4. Cheer for yourself first.

The great writer and commentator, Touré, tells a story about being invited to Kanye West's house. As he walked inside Kanye's home, he saw a big, giant poster of Kanye right inside the living room. Touré asked the question we all are thinking right now. "Kanye, why do you have a giant picture of yourself on the wall?"

Kanye responded, "Well, I got to cheer for me before anyone can cheer for me."[1]

What a fantastic response. Love yourself like Kanye loves Kanye.

When Jesus was asked what the greatest commandments were in Matthew 22:34-40, His second response was to "Love your neighbor as you love yourself." It starts with loving God, continues with loving you, and ends with loving people. Many of us choose not to love what God has created in us, but here He is saying, "Love yourself. Only then can you love others."

One of the most important discoveries in life is recognizing the value within you. You have everything you need to begin maximizing the life you were given to lead. You've got the goods. It is time to develop what you are made of. Capitalize on the traits that make the difference by recognizing the pure value you have inside of you.

When you recognize your value, you add value to the world.

ACKNOWLEDGMENTS

To my parents, Marvin and Bonnie Cox. Thank you for loving me unconditionally and training me in the way I should go. Anything good that I say or do is in large part because I'm standing on the shoulders of giants. You are the heroes in my story.

To my pastor and friend, Joel Scrivner. Thank you for taking a chance on me when I was a raw 18-year-old kid. You saw potential in me that others didn't. Thank you for investing in me all these years. We are tied together for life.

To my family. You have been a constant strength and encouragement to me. Your support on this journey has been overwhelming.

To our church staff. The roots of this message started in a staff meeting devotion. I love being on the team with you.

To my friends Steven Washington and Cassius Miller. Thank you for letting me talk all these ideas out as I was writing this book. You both were pillars to me in this process.

To Simon and Tebra Kolath. My wife and I call you friends, but you feel like family. We've been on this journey for 12 years and I'm grateful for the safe haven we have in your home.

To Ryan Leak. You were the first person I told about this book idea, after Angelmarie. You told me, "You're not too young, you're too old. It's time to get started." Thank you for being someone I can model after and look up to.

To my Legendary Youth family. We were together for a decade and I wouldn't trade my time with you for anything. You have made an indelible mark on my life.

To Amy Noelck. Wow, am I glad Ryan recommended you to me. You have been the best editor to work with. You have helped me so much in this process. Thank you for your excellence and the heart you put into this book.

To Remi Sullivan. Your creative spark has been a massive help in this project. Thank you so much for adding your design to this book. There's no one better at this than you.

To you, the reader. I wrote these words for you. Oftentimes, I sat at my kitchen table with natural light beaming through as I typed these words. I hope you leave this book better than when you came. Recognize your value.

NOTES

INTRODUCTION – RECOGNIZING YOUR VALUE
1. Lusko, Levi. *Eyes of a Lion* (W Publishing Group, Thomas Nelson, 2015), 176-177.
2. Cain, Susan. *Quiet* (Random House Inc, 2013), 241.

CHAPTER ONE – YOU ARE VALUABLE
1. Maxwell, John. *25 Ways to Win with People* (Thomas Nelson, 2005), 7-8.
2. Humes, James. *Speak Like Churchill, Stand Like Lincoln* (Three Rivers Press, New York, New York, 2002), 186.
3. Lusko, Levi. *Eyes of a Lion* (W Publishing Group, Thomas Nelson, 2015), 1-2.
4. Batterson, Mark. *All In* (ZONDERVAN, 2013), 157.
5. Maxwell, John. *25 Ways to Win with People* (Thomas Nelson, 2005), 4-5.

CHAPTER TWO – USE YOUR VOICE
1. Batterson, Mark. *The Circle Maker* (ZONDERVAN, 2011, 2016), 69-70.

CHAPTER THREE – YOU CAN'T TEACH DESIRE
1. Lazenby, Roland. *The Life* (Full Court Press, 2014), 515.

CHAPTER FOUR – STAND FIRM

CHAPTER FIVE – FEAR VS. FAITH
1. Berginer, Vladimir and Cohen, Chaim. *"The Nature of Goliath's Visual Disorder and the Actual Role of His Personal Bodyguard,"* Ancient Near Eastern Studies (2006), 43.

CHAPTER SIX – DESIRABLE DIFFICULTIES
1. Bjork, E. L., and Bjork, R. A. *Making Things Hard On Yourself, But In A Good Way: Creating Desirable Difficulties To Enhance Learning.* In M. A. Gernsbacher, R. W. Pew, L. M. Hough, J. R. Pomerantz (Eds.) & FABBS Foundation, Psychology and the Real World: Essays Illustrating

NOTES

Fundamental Contributions to Society (New York, NY, US: Worth Publishers, 2011), Chapter 5.

2. Gladwell, Malcolm. *David and Goliath* (Little, Brown and Company Hachette Book Group, 2013), 129.

3. Maxwell, John. *Winning with People* (Thomas Nelson, 2004), 243-244.

4. Logan, Julie. *Dyslexic Entrepreneurs: The Incidence; Their Coping Strategies and Their Business Skills* (2009), Dyslexia, 4:328-46.

5. Gladwell, Malcolm. *David and Goliath* (Little, Brown and Company Hachette Book Group, 2013), 113.

6. Eisenstadt, Marvin. *Parental Loss and Genius* (American Psychological Association, 1978), American Psychologist.

7. McWhorter, Diane. *Carry Me Home: Birmingham, Alabama; The Climatic Battle of the Civil Rights Revolution* (Touchstone 2002).

CHAPTER SEVEN – PREPARATION

1. Ferriss, Timothy. *Tribe of Mentors* (Houghton Mifflin Harcourt Publishing Company, 2017), 98.

2. Cowherd, Colin. *"The Herd."* October 5, 2018.

3. Tibbetts, Graham. *Key That Could Have Saved the Titanic* (The Telegraph, 2007),
https://www.telegraph.co.uk/news/uknews/1561604/Key-that-could-have-saved-the-Titanic.html. Web. December 2018.

4. Peterson, Jordan B. *12 Rules for Life* (Random House Canada, 2018), 157.

5. Ferriss, Timothy. *Tools of Titans* (Houghton Mifflin Harcourt Publishing Company, 2017), 130-131.

6. Batterson, Mark. *Play the Man* (Baker Books, 2017), 18.

7. Ferriss, Timothy. *Tools of Titans* (Houghton Mifflin Harcourt Publishing Company, 2017), 211.

CHAPTER EIGHT – LEADERSHIP

1. Morris, Edward. *The Rise of Theodore Roosevelt* (New York: Random House, 2010).

2. Batchelor, Doug. *The Beginning of Wisdom* (Lightsource, 2018),
https://www.lightsource.com/ministry/amazing-facts/articles/the-beginning-of-wisdom-14923.html. Web. December 2018.

3. Mansfield, Stephen. *Book of Manly Men* (Nelson Books, Thomas Nelson, 2013), 139-140.

NOTES

4. Reber, Paul. *What is the Memory Capacity of the Human Brain?* (Scientific American, 2010), http://www.scientificamerican.com/article/what-is-the-memory-capacity. Web. December 2018.

5. Dalio, Ray. *Principles* (Simon & Schuster, 2017), 96.

6. Stolberg, Sheryl Gay. *"Year After Katrina, Bush Still Fights for 9/11 Image,"* New York Times, August 28, 2006.

7. Humes, James. *Speak Like Churchill, Stand Like Lincoln* (Three Rivers Press, New York, New York, 2002), 185-186.

CHAPTER NINE – EXCELLENCE

1. Batterson, Mark. *Play the Man* (Baker Books, 2017), 76.

2. Mansfield, Stephen. *Book of Manly Men* (Nelson Books, Thomas Nelson, 2013), 161.

3. Stockstill, Larry. *10 Helpful Things All Pastors Should Know* (Larry Stockstill, 2018), https://www.larrystockstill.com/blog/10-helpful-things-pastors-know. Web. December 2018

4. Batterson, Mark. *Play the Man* (Baker Books, 2017).

5. Isaacson, Walter. *Steve Jobs* (Simon & Schuster, 2011), 467.

CHAPTER TEN – RELATIONSHIPS

1. Dalrock. *The Husband Store* (Dalrock, 2010) https://dalrock.wordpress.com/2010/08/16/the-husband-store/. Web. December 2018.

2. Thompson, Alice. Help Kids to Kick Social Media Addiction (The Times UK, 2018), https://www.thetimes.co.uk/article/help-kids-to-kick-social-media-addiction-x7xjqh9rf. Web. December 2018.

3. Bell, Rob. *Sex God* (Harper One, 2007, 2012).

CHAPTER ELEVEN – INVESTING IN OTHERS

1. Greany, Ed, Hecht, Walter, and Walker, Douglas. *Lawn Chair Larry* (Darwin Awards, 2012), https://darwinawards.com/stupid/stupid1998-11.html. Web. December 2018.

CHAPTER TWELVE – CONCLUSION

1. Ferriss, Timothy. *Tools of Titans* (Houghton Mifflin Harcourt Publishing Company, 2017), 221, story told by Morgan Spurlock.

AUTHOR BIO

Brandon Cox is on the pastoral team of Oaks Church in McKinney, Texas. He is a vibrant communicator with over twelve years of experience. He and his wife, Angelmarie, reside in the DFW area.

BRANDONJCOX.COM

59515196R00133

Made in the USA
Columbia, SC
04 June 2019